From the
MAGIC OF THE WATERWAYS
to the
CHALLENGE OF THE SEA
by
Yocky Lol Gilson
Part 1
THE RUNT'S PROGRESS

The Runt's Progress
by Yocky Lol Gilson

Published by
PB Software
3 Nelson Road
Ashingdon, Rochford
Essex SS4 3EJ

FIRST EDITION
First Printing September2010

A CIP catalogue record of this book
is available from the British Library

ISBN 978-0-9565891-5-6

PREFACE

The twelve thousand ton cargo ship came crashing out of the dense black fog. Her engines throbbed like distant thunder and her bow-wave hung over the *Ros Beara* full of menace and with a roar similar to a raging water-fall, I had just five seconds to re-act and take what little evasive action was possible in the very limited amount of time available. We had already made one good haul and the port deck was full of Cod, Herrings and Sprats. The starboard deck was stacked with a hundred fish trays, some already filled with quivering Herrings. I spun the wheel hard to starboard in an attempt to stop the ships bow-wave actually coming a-board and to cushion the impact if the two vessels did collide. I was not quick enough! The water smashed onto the port deck washing fish over-board and throwing the three crew 'that were sorting the fish' into the scuppers. At that precise moment I was certain that the *Ros Beara's* days were numbered and that my fantastic life as a trawler skipper was about to end. We are towing a ten fathom pelagic mid-water pair trawl over the tide ten miles west of the Edinburgh channels in the Thames Estuary. My brother Ray skippers the vessel towing the other side of the net and the huge merchant ship is between us. We cannot see each-other, the fog is much too thick. We are crazy, but these are the risks we are prepared to take in order to survive as professional trawlermen in the Thames Estuary and English Channel

CHAPTER ONE

In spite of the fact that it was still quite early the sun beat down relentlessly. It was June 1940. Three children each carrying a small case or bag containing most of their belongings, plus a gas mask slung from the shoulder, headed for the railway station in company with many others.

A waiting train was to take them to an unknown destination in the Midlands away from a war which was raging over half the world. Invasion across the English Channel by German forces appeared inevitable and could happen any day.

Laurie Gilson, his elder sister Doreen and her best friend Jean, were among several hundreds who had left their parents, not knowing if they would ever see them again.

Conditions for travelling could not have been worse as they were herded aboard the train. Each carriage packed to capacity with thirsty children, who had been instructed not to take any form of drink as this would be provided.

It was obvious from the start that the very hot conditions had not been catered for. Water was in short supply. Many of the children were already sick either from fright or the over-crowded situation in the carriages. There was an atmosphere of abject misery and confusion surrounding all concerned and the train had not yet left the station!

At last the enormous engine sounded its whistle and the nightmare journey began. The train pulled slowly out of the station in fact it continued to move slowly all day and although the destination was less than two hundred miles away, it took more than seven hours to complete.

The train stopped many times for reasons unknown to the children, but they were well aware that each mile covered, took them further away from the parents they loved. The sultry air was heavy with doubt and a sense of despair. Most of the children were bewildered with the speed and course of events which had taken place in just a few short months.

Doreen and Jean paid little attention to Laurie. They were six years older and far more mature. They did make some attempt to cheer him up, but getting little response, gave up in despair. He could not blame them. He showed very little interest in anything. He was a frail, quiet almost dwarf like little boy and although eight years old had received hardly any schooling, due to the fact that he had been plagued with illness.

Life had really only started for Laurie a few months before when an operation had been carried out on his throat. He had lived a very sheltered life and was considered to be his mother's pet because of the care and attention she had shown him. There was no doubt that survival was due entirely to the fact that she had nursed him day and night, quite apart from looking after the other four boys and two girls which made up her family, and of course Father.

Laurie was the youngest boy and the fact that he had survived did on the face of it appear to make him a bit special. At the present moment he was slumped in the corner of this dirty horrible carriage, silent and alone with his thoughts. He had been sat on, jumped on and pushed about by the bigger boys, but was to miserable to care, illness had made him something of a loner.

The fact that he could neither read or write a single letter had left him way behind and out in the cold. He was considered to be a dunce and rather a joke with the teachers - a boy beyond redemption.

At this moment he was seated with his eyes closed, not knowing or caring what it was all about. He was not an unfriendly boy, in fact the last few months had seen a dramatic change in his life. He had come to realize that many sports came naturally to him due to the fact that he had a keen eye and a natural sense of timing. He loved to kick or thump a ball with anything he could get hold of but because he was so far behind in his school work usually played alone, the very thought of what awaited him at the end of this journey made him shudder, perhaps he would soon wake up and find that it had all been a bad dream.

The sound of cheering broke into his thoughts! Word had come round that they were nearing there destination and all the children wanted to look out of the window. Once more Laurie was being squashed but at least the nightmare train ride was nearly over.

As the engine came to a grinding halt, its brakes screeched so loudly that it sounded as if the engine itself was laughing at his predicament.

Teachers were already walking up and down the station platform shouting out orders for the children to stay where they were until told to leave the train. Several doors had been opened and boys were spilling out of the carriages, only to be pushed back by harassed teachers who were almost at breaking point after such a trying day.

Although the train journey was at an end the teachers problems were far from over. The children lined up to march out of the station and it soon became obvious that this was not their final destination.

As it turned out, they were only about three miles from the town that was to be their home for some considerable time but Laurie had no way of knowing this. The thought of so many miles already covered since early morning he began to lose all sense of time and direction. The sight of many different coloured buses waiting to take him even further away from the home he loved did nothing to dispel his fears, in fact it only served to increase the misery.

He had always been known as a dreamer and now as the children climbed into the buses, his mind wandered back to

Southend-On-Sea where a penny ride on the tram had always been accepted as a reward for good behaviour. He was not allowed to bask in the safety of his dream for long.

The buses were quickly filling up and there was no choice other than to follow the herd of stamping, screaming youngsters as they raced up the stairs of each double decker bus fighting to get the best seats. Each child had been counted onto the buses by teachers in charge of their own specific group and after much conferring they appeared satisfied that all were present and correct.

At last the convoy began to move off, this was the last stage of the journey and as it turned out for Laurie by far the most pleasant. Sitting on the top deck of the bus he had a good commanding view of a very green and pretty countryside. Nottinghamshire, hilly and quite heavily wooded, was a drastic and rather lovely change from the flat ground of Essex, which was his home county.

For the next ten or fifteen minutes he felt a little more relaxed and even began to enjoy the ride but it was only a temporary feeling and not likely to last as he knew from experience.

Gradually the country-side began to disappear as the line of buses rolled into the midland town of Sutton in Ashfield.

They finally came to a halt at the end of an unmade road which led up to the entrance of Hardwick Street School. One of the older boys sarcastically remarked, 'A human sorting centre!' Laurie looked doubtfully at the dark forbidding place. His feelings about such buildings were not good but for the moment his thoughts were distracted by the people lining either side of the road who had come to welcome the children. Thinking about it he realized they must have been waiting for ages. The train's arrival was way behind time and the warm welcome now given the children made him feel a little more easy inside - maybe things would not be so bad after all.

There was a great deal of pushing and shoving going on in order to be first in line for the billets. Laurie tripped over his case falling hard on the rough ground and blood from his right knee began to flow freely down into his sock. It was probably a surprise to the onlookers who might have expected tears but he pulled a grubby piece of rag from his pocket, wiped the blood away and carried on as if nothing had happened. The people might have thought that this little kid was tougher than he looked but Laurie was just past caring. His misery was complete.

It soon became obvious that in some cases up to three children were being taken into some homes. This meant that Laurie was able to stay with his sister Doreen and her friend Jean. The two girls were introduced to their hostess,, a lady named Mrs. Conners, and her two children Sue and Ben. Mrs. Conners turned out to be a very strict but kind person. Her husband had been one of the first to be called up for military service and was away at the war, this made it possible for her to take all three children into her home. Indeed she welcomed the extra work and the small allowance for each child would be a great help.

Introductions completed, Mrs. Conners could see that her new charges were very tired and more than ready for some food and sleep. After a light meal and a milky cup of tea she quickly ushered them upstairs to the bedroom.

Thinking that he had been forgotten Laurie sat down very gently on the enormous bed which gave the impression of filling the whole room. He was staring vacantly into space as the girls began to undress, They were so busy talking they had forgotten all about him, then Mary suddenly realizing that he was there and thinking that he was watching them, promptly clipped him round the ear telling him not to be a rude little boy. Laurie was baffled, to him at that moment in time boys and girls were all the same! Why all the fuss?

Several hours passed and although he lay with eyes tightly closed he was unable to sleep. Laurie tried to cuddle up to his sister but she pushed him roughly away, so laying on his back he opened his eyes, trying to see the cracks in the ceiling that he had noticed while it was still light but the room was too dark. He tried to imagine himself back home with his mother and thinking about her the tears began to roll down his cheeks. He was a miserable lonely little boy. At last, mercifully, helpless and exhausted, Laurie sunk into oblivion.

CHAPTER TWO

Laurie awoke the following morning to the sound of cheering. He looked around thinking he must still be dreaming. The unfamiliar room and the strange noises coming from outside. It was several minutes before all the happenings of the previous day came flooding back to him.

It must be quite late for there was no sign of Mary and Jean. Jumping out of bed he ran to the window and threw it open. Outside, what appeared to be a rather rough game of rounders, was being played. About twenty boys were involved in the game, but it was the girls lined up on either side of the street who were creating all the noise.

Laurie could feel the excitement mounting inside his slightly built frame just at the thought of getting into that game. Throwing on his clothes as fast as was humanly possible, stopping neither to wash or eat breakfast which had been prepared for him by Mrs. Conners, he dashed out into the street. Just as he arrived on the scene Ben Conners (from the house where he had slept) reached up and caught the ball one handed above his head, and shouted "That's it, unless we let one of them bat again, it's our game." Laurie sat down on the kerb, filled with disappointment.

Ben Conner could not have been more unlike Laurie. He was thirteen years old, well built and thick set, with a crop of thick black curly hair and friendly face, also as it turned out leader of the local kids. The game being played was against the new-comers from the south.

There was a certain amount of tension between the two

groups of youngsters. They were about equal in numbers but very different in so many ways. From the south there were many more girls than boys and several of them were much older and obviously thought they were in command. Despite this fact, there was no way the boys from the north were going to allow them to take part in the game. In their environment the boys had no doubt what-so-ever that they reigned supreme.

One or two of the older girls had suggested that they be allowed to take part in the game to make up the numbers, only to be met with snorts of contempt from the northern team. They were having no sissy girls getting mixed up in their sports, this game was only for the men and that was that.

Ben turned and walked over to one of his mates who had been bowling, or rather throwing the ball at whoever was batting. "Hey, Skinny" said Ben "the other side are a player short." Skinny, obviously so named because he was tall and very thin. "Maybe" he said "but no one can bat twice, that's the rules, so we win by three points."

Ben was a nice lad and very fair minded, "They should have another batsman," he said, looking up and down the street. It was then that he spotted Laurie "Hey, Littl'un, fancy you can save your team," he said with a smile on his face. "He'll get hurt" said Skinny, "he's too small."

Before there could be any more argument, Laurie was up on his feet heading for the piece of tree trunk which they called a bat. Grabbing it with both hands he stood looking defiantly at Skinny. The street had gone strangely quiet, all the shouting and cheering had stopped

The game had been played in a friendly atmosphere, both sides wanted their team to win but no one wanted to see this scrawny little kid get hurt. "It's not going to make much difference anyway," said Skinny, winding his bowling arm round so hard it looked as if he might take off. Laurie was terrified but tried not to let it show. "Don't take any notice of him, kid," said Ben laughing, "just knock him over the mill wall and your side wins - it's a rounder if you top the wall."

Laurie stood waiting, the stump of tree in his hands was only rough cut but well balanced, it felt good. He hoped Skinny might be getting tired and would run out of energy before he bowled but when the ball did come it was so fast and low he barely saw it, Ben said "Strike one!"

Laurie had a good eye and a natural sense of timing, If only Skinny would bowl a bit higher. He had two more chances. The next ball went past just the same and Laurie made no stroke Ben called "Strike two!" - there was a moan from the spectators.

Skinny must have come to the conclusion that it was a mere formality and although the last ball was just as fast, it came through waist high.

Laurie swung the bat with all his might and there was a loud sweet crack. Skinny stood watching in disbelief as the ball cleared the mill wall with plenty to spare. The girls cheered with delight and Laurie had never felt so good. He felt even better when Ben came across and put his arm round his shoulder and hugged him. That was the beginning of a great friendship.

Laurie may have been the hero of 'The Street,' but it was a completely different story the next day at school. Unfortunately, although Hardwick Street School was new to him, the teacher, Mrs. Clark was not. A new special class had been formed, all twenty five boys coming from Southend-On-Sea.

One or two he recognized and had in fact been at school with before but only for brief periods, due to his poor health he was seldom there. The sight of Mrs. Clark, this little grey haired teacher, scared the life out of him, He had no doubt whatsoever that he was in for trouble. After the register had been called, Mrs. Clark looked round the class at the boys, her steely grey eyes making a note of each face, she knew them all. "Get out your reading books you will find them in the desks, "I intend to hear each one of you read," Laurie's heart sank. "Gilson come to the front and bring your book." The moment Laurie was dreading had arrived and there was no escape. "Commence to read at page one first chapter," said the teacher. Laurie stared blankly at the open book, he was helpless and unable to read even one word. The other children sniggered. "It's not funny," snapped Mrs. Clark, "this boy never learns anything. He's bone idle."

The unlikely appearance of Mrs. Clark had taken Laurie completely by surprise. At least a new teacher, prepared to listen to his problems, might have given him the chance to make a fresh start, but now once again he would be lost in a world of learning which had no meaning, he was quite innocent but nevertheless he felt very guilty. It turned out to be a typical school morning for Laurie, trouble seemed to follow him around. Even when speaking to the boy in the next desk, trying to get some assistance, Mrs. Clark noticed and called him to the front of the class. Gave him a rap across the knuckles with her ruler, she then made him kneel for twenty minutes in the corner of the classroom. This played havoc with his knees and did nothing for his education.

At last play time came, much to Lauries' relief. It was good to feel the fresh air on his face as he ran out on the playing field which adjoined Hardwick Street School. The school was really meant for senior boys only and was well equipped. It had a large gymnasium plus two football pitches, leaving plenty of grass for other activities of which there were many.

In one corner Laurie found Ben Conners, many of the bigger boys carried the smaller ones (mostly from Laurie's own class) on their backs. The game was piggy back fighting and although rather dangerous looked great fun.

It was not long before Ben noticed that Laurie had arrived on the scene and came running over, "Come on kid, jump on my back, let's show em," and soon they were in the thick of the fighting, trying to pull the other horse and riders to the ground. The bad time in class was soon forgotten.

Ben turned out to be a pretty tough character and by the time they both lay on the ground gasping for breath. There were not many left standing.

The boys sat smiling at each other, they were so different, yet a bond of friendship was developing between them which neither could fully understand. Even their language at first sounded different, although of course it was just the dialect.

In spite of the fact that Ben was a senior and nearly five years older than Laurie he found great pleasure in showing this small boy from the south of England round his home town. In the days and weeks that followed they explored just about everything this very typical midland town had to offer.

One of the most fascinating pastimes for Laurie was playing in the old cotton mills of which there were many, he had never seen anything like them before. There was certainly nothing to compare with these dark, empty, mysterious old buildings in the town he came from and they would spend hours searching among the broken looms and thousands of cotton reels that lay everywhere.

They would throw stones at the few windows that remained whole, climb the high walls and swing hand over hand along guttering, drain pipes and roof beams. There was always something different to do.

The months passed by and Lauries stay at Hardwick Street, although getting off to a bad start with Mrs. Clark, was not too unhappy. The ferocious little lady continued to harass and intimidate him whenever she got the chance and because of this his education made little or no progress. Ben's friendship outside the classroom, pleasantly protective and usually around when trouble threatened made the months at the school much happier than Laurie could ever have imagined, so it was with much trepidation regarding his future that Laurie received the news that he was to have another billet and also a new school. When the dreaded day arrived, Laurie his sister Mary and her friend Jean, said their good-by's. Ben was there to see them leave and assured Laurie that the other side of town was not that far and that they would see each other soon. As the three children walked down the street waving to Mrs. Conners and her family, they knew different.

CHAPTER FOUR

Mrs. Conners, for her part, had a tear in her eye as she watched the children disappear from sight. She determined to write to the parents with an idea which had been growing in her mind, but this was something the children would not know about for some time. That letter when it was posted, changed the course of quite a few lives. The lady, a Mrs. Vange, who had arrived to guide the children across town to their new billet, chatted with the girls in a friendly manner, she was a talkative plump little person and loved to know everyone's business.

Laurie didn't take too much interest in the conversation but during many hours spent in Ben's company, he had become much more aware of life and all the different things that were happening outside of his own small world. He gathered that he was the cause of them having to change homes and the girls made it very obvious that they were most unhappy about it.

He remembered that his class took a test some weeks previous, and the rumour that Mrs. Clark was leaving. This had been a great relief to him but the fact that the special class was to be broken up and each boy would move to the school of his own age group together with pupils of similar intelligence, had not occurred to Laurie until later. It had upset the girls very badly, he gathered at the moment he was most unpopular.

All the streets and houses seemed the same, row upon row of red brick terraced buildings with tunnelled entrances in each one. Laurie assumed these strange side entrances were made to allow the men who came at night (with masks on their faces) to empty the large toilet tanks which were housed inside a wooden shed at the back of the little houses. There were no sewage drains laid at that time. At least not in that particular part of town.

When at last they arrived at their destination, a rather tall, slim, pretty young woman answered the door. She smiled rather thinly but bade them enter. The lady who had accompanied the three children across town addressed her as Mrs. Slack. They soon realized that Mrs. Slack's husband was away in the army fighting the war and she had accepted the evacuees on the conditions that it would not be for too long a period. As it turned out later, She was not an unkind person but a very poor cook and quite unused to children or housework. Nevertheless, she was prepared to do her best for her young guests. So having said farewell to their escort once more they were shown into a rather smart newly decorated bedroom. Mrs. Slack leaving them alone to take care of themselves.

Laurie, as usual turned his back on the girls and began to undress but the girls had other ideas. He was down to just his underpants, which he slept in when the girls pounced on him. It was clear that sensing the lack of discipline, they intended wreaking their vengeance on Laurie who they blamed for having to change billets. Taken completely by surprise, he was thrown on the bed and his pants were pulled off. The girls jumped on top of him prodding him with their fists and tickling all over his body.

Laurie fought back, he was no longer the frail, weak little boy who had left his mother months before. The time spent with Ben Conners had toughened him considerably, he had become more sturdy and was well into his tenth year. Now as he wrestled with the girls it was their turn to be surprised. Mary fell out of bed helped by a push from Laurie's foot and Jean' who had been kneeling on top suddenly found herself underneath, her arms were pinned above her head and Laurie, stark naked, Lay full length on top.

It all happened in seconds. In the struggle Jean's dress had risen up round her waist, pressed against her soft thighs Laurie felt his body begin to stiffen, something that had never happened to him before was taking charge of his body. He wanted to press harder against the warm flesh but instinct and a feeling of guilt made him pull back. He jumped off the bed trying to hide himself.

The room had gone very quiet, both Jean and Mary understood what had happened but remained silent, undressed, and got into bed. That was the last time all three slept together.

In the days that followed Laurie tried not to think about the incident in the bedroom with Jean, he still had the feeling of guilt but that surge of energy which pulsed through his veins, made him feel so good he was sure it was something quite natural. The holiday quickly passed, after which he joined Priestly Road School. They were still living with Mrs. Slack but Laurie now slept in a room on his own and with this he was content.

CHAPTER FIVE

At assembly on the first morning of school, Mr. Sloan, the headmaster, told the boys in his opening speech that while he was headmaster as long as every boy worked hard they would all have the same opportunity. He would help each one as much as he could, Laurie determined he would do his best but he also realized that without special help, for him there could be no chance.

Fortunately for Laurie as it turned out, the school had its own football field and he had grown to love the game. He stayed at school to lunch, only taking about twenty minutes to eat, the other one hour he was on the field playing football. He revelled in the game and although at the time he could not have known this, it was seriously going to help him in his studies.

Laurie's teacher was a Miss Redfern, a very kind lady and in her day a very good teacher but soon due for retirement. She knew Laurie tried at his lessons, but he appeared to make little progress, she was sorry it was not in her power to help him. She made up her mind to speak to Mr. Jones the teacher who was to take her place.

On Miss Redfern's last day before retirement, Laurie entered the classroom, walked to his desk and sat down. The desks were in pairs and the boy in the next seat was a boy named Stafford. He was great, he and Laurie become good friends but he was a real practical joker. On this particular morning he had put a drawing pin on Laurie's chair, who sat down quite unsuspecting but quickly rose with a loud cry of pain. Miss Redfern called Laurie to the front. "What was all that noise about," she queried. "Sorry Miss, I sat down with a bump." Miss Redfern suspected otherwise but wisely let it go. "Return to your seat and please don't disrupt the class." Staf, as he was known smiled and said "Thanks," as Laurie sat down. "Don't worry," said Laurie "I'll get my revenge on the field at lunch time.

Miss Redfern had her retirement party and left the school. Laurie had liked Miss Redfern and was genuinely sorry to see her go. He had made little or no progress in her class but she had been the first teacher who had tried to understand his problems. She was a nice lady and he was going to miss her.

The next day Mr. Sloan the headmaster was in charge of the class until lunch-time. The boys ate their dinner quickly and as usual headed for the football field. The one hour at lunchtime playing football meant everything to Laurie, all his energy and enthusiasm went into the game and in some measure made up for his failure in class.

Today, as usual, the boys were completely engrossed in the game. No one had noticed the slim, grey haired athletic looking man who stood on the touch-line watching with interest as the boys played. The grey hair was nearer white but one only had to look into those clear keen eyes to realize he was not that old, a very commanding figure well over six feet tall.

It was not an unusual occurrence to have spectators, the field ran parallel with a main road. Often quite a number of people would gather to enjoy the energetic antics of the youngsters at play. The boys, oblivious to everything but the game, had no idea that the man was anything special. They had no way of knowing that the person taking such a keen interest in there game was Mr. Jones, their future schoolmaster. He was a great lover of most sports but far more important than this as Laurie would learn in the future, he was an excellent teacher.

Mr. Jones made it his business to know what motivated each boy and took a personal interest in their home-life and background. One lad in particular had claimed his attention. The boy was not very big and still had a great deal of growing to do but it was his complete involvement and enthusiasm to be in the game all the time. It was his boundless energy which made Mr. Jones smile.

He turned away and disappeared in the direction of the school just as the bell clanged to signal the end of lunchtime. At the sound of the bell some thirty boys made their way back over the bridge and into school still discussing the game. They were fortunate that only the width of the railway separated school from playing fields, just a two minute walk.

Later, as they entered the classroom, there was an air of expectancy, all eyes were searching for the new teacher but he was nowhere to be seen, the room was empty. Laurie sat down at his desk and Staf soon joined him. They talked about the game that had just finished and about football in general. Staf was saying how much better it would be if they all had football boots - not one of them had ever owned or even worn real football boots. Such things were in short supply because of the war but even if they had been available it was doubtful if any of these boys could have afforded them.

As the war had progressed almost every family had been affected in one way or another. The boys quite often discussed together how their fathers or elder brothers and sisters were faring away from home, it was the one thing they all had in common. The noise gradually increased, few heard or noticed the door open and close behind Mr. Jones as he entered the room. He walked quietly across to his desk four bamboo canes tucked under his arm.

Suddenly the room was silent, every boys attention focused on the canes and the teacher in that order. Every move that Mr. Jones made was slow and deliberate, each cane was carefully examined and laid on the desk in line side by side. Lifting the lid he placed the canes inside, lowered the lid and faced the class.

There was an audible gulp from several dry throats - the

teacher had arrived! Just in those few fleeting seconds which elapsed between the time Mr. Jones closed his desk and the moment he began to speak, Laurie's mind raced through time, back over the last five years. The first two virtually without schooling, after that a succession of teachers, some of whom would have liked to help him given the time but failed due to the large number of pupils in each class.

Then there were teachers like Mrs. Clark, who completely failed to understand his predicament at all, convincing themselves that they were just dealing with a lazy boy who had very little to offer and absolutely no interest in learning.

Laurie came back to the present with a start, once again he was faced with a new teacher, a total stranger who had the power to determine his future. The choice of trying to help him or leaving him to sink even deeper into the desolation of not being able to read or write, a boy whose mind became a complete blank when asked to add together even the most simple numbers. Laurie studied the teacher's face looking for a glimmer of hope but preparing himself for another long term of misery in the classroom.

Mr. Jones opened the register and began to speak in a crisp clear voice. Slowly he worked his way through the list of names in front of him, looking up to form a mental picture of each boy as they answered "Yes Sir." There was a pause as the teacher, very much at ease and taking his time, returned the dark red ledger to the desk. Laurie waited for the words he had grown to dread over the last two or three years, they were usually "Get out your reading book," or "The first lesson this afternoon will be." And from that moment on Laurie could always expect trouble. Mr. Jones did neither of these things he sat back in his chair and relaxed!

That afternoon was the first time in his life that Laurie enjoyed school. The new teacher was definitely different. He went round the class talking to each boy in turn about their families who, if any were away at the war, what was their favourite sport. He asked which of the three major subjects, reading, writing, or arithmetic did they enjoy the most, and if this was also their strongest subject. Laurie listened, following every word, He was learning things about his classmates, interesting things, lots of things he had never known before. He was so absorbed while the teacher was speaking to his friend Staf, that when Mr. Jones said "Well Gilson what about you?" For a moment he was lost for words. Then Laurie taking a deep breath said "I love all sports Sir, but I hate most lessons." All the boys burst out laughing and the teacher smiled but Laurie continued, he told how he had missed his first two and a half years schooling. As a result of this he was so far behind the other boys of his own age, he never had the chance to learn. The teacher stopped Laurie at that point and carried on round the class until he had spoken to every pupil.

The afternoon came to an end and everyone made for the door, Mr. Jones called "Not you Gilson, stay behind I want to have a little chat." Laurie's heart sunk once more, he was in for trouble again. "Laurie I want to help you." Laurie could hardly believe his ears, to be addressed on Christian name terms by a teacher was something of an honour. Usually reserved for a teacher's favourite, Laurie had never been that.

Mr. Jones went on to say that he had examined all the class work books and realized just how backward Laurie was. There was no disputing the fact that he was well behind the other boys, "But," Mr. Jones said, "if you are prepared to put as much effort into your work as you put into that game of football this morning, We shall get on fine."

Laurie, still somewhat dazed promised to try and was promptly given his first homework. This homework consisted of a ring of numbers like a clock face but all mixed up, The idea being to add up the numbers going clockwise and then reverse and go anti-clockwise, not stopping when the circle had been completed but to go on as long as possible.

For the next three weeks Laurie stuck doggedly to his task of counting the numbers, at first he found it very difficult but he wanted to please this new teacher who had so strangely taken an interest in him. Every couple of days he would be asked by Mr. Jones to stay behind for a short time after the other boys had gone home, just to check on his progress and give advice if it was needed.

Much to Laurie' surprise he began to enjoy the exercise, sure enough his ability to count and add up improved tremendously. Although at the time he did not notice, his speed at adding numbers increased with every day. The teacher did not worry him with other subjects but allowed him to concentrate all day on the circle of numbers. Laurie was quite content to do so.

There was a growing respect for Mr. Jones. The canes were soon forgotten, behaviour in class was good, mainly because the boys had been kept interested and busy since the day he had arrived.

On this particular Monday morning, as the boys came into class, Mr. Jones was writing a circle of numbers on the blackboard. After the usual roll call and good mornings had been said, he called their attention to the board. "We are going to concentrate on addition, in fact mental arithmetic," he went on. "You always sit in your four teams and you are going to compete against each other in teams, then as individuals." He walked across the room with a ruler in his hand, Pointing to the circle, started to move slowly round the numbers. I will set the speed, you will add and count out loud. The whole class will do the exercise several times before we start to compete."

It sounded simple enough, the boys began to chant in time with the tap of the ruler, They would not be stopped as long as one voice kept up the speed and gave correct answers. Laurie now realized the value of all the concentration on his part and gentle tuition from Mr. Jones - together they shared that morning of triumph. At the close of the contest Laurie ran out a clear winner. At least in one subject he was top of the class, much to the amazement of all present, that is all apart from Mr. Jones, who went for his lunch break a very contented teacher.

CHAPTER SIX

Life for Laurie had now taken on a different meaning and although he still greatly missed his parents, the rest of his family and that great longing for the sea that would always be with him, he was becoming more involved with all the activities that went on at school.

He continued to make slow but steady progress with his studies, thanks entirely to Mr. Jones, who also joined with the boys at lunchtime football and although nearly fifty years of age was still a very fit man. Popular, strict, but scrupulously fair. Priestly Road School was proving to be a happy one for Laurie.

As time went by and thoughts of Mrs. Conners and Ben began to fade. The three children settled in quite comfortably with Mrs. Slack who, when she had become accustomed to having the girl's company, grew very fond of them and was in no hurry to see them leave.

Meanwhile, back in Laurie's home town on the south coast, lots of things were happening. Father, who was a professional fisherman, had received two letters in the same week. He had served in the first world war but was just over the age limit to enlist when the present war had begun. The first of the two letters was an official request, asking if he would be prepared to work on the Grand Union Canal. His task was to Skipper two Barges that were going from the Midlands down to London carrying coal on a regular basis. The second letter came from Mrs. Conners saying that her father who lived alone, would be only too pleased for them to share his house, if they wished to be re-united with their family in Sutton in Ashfield. The offer was promptly accepted.

Soon the whole of Laurie's family, apart from two older brothers who were serving in the Royal Navy, came together again in Sutton in Ashfield and although Father spent much of his time away on the Canal Barges, every few weeks the family joined in a united weekend.

Laurie was kept informed of all these events by his sister Mary, who would now be leaving school and looking for a job, whilst her friend Jean would be returning home to her parents, also to commence work, their school life was finished.

Laurie of course was pleased to be living with his mother once again, but it also meant other changes. From their new home he now had a two mile walk every morning and evening to and from school. As things turned out, there was another very large school named Hillocks, close by his new home, Laurie had no wish to leave Priestly Road, where he was popular and very happy.

Mr. Jones, the teacher for whom he had so much respect was now helping him with his reading, which was still very poor. These problems as it turned out all took care of themselves. Laurie was now ten years old and the Christmas holidays were approaching. It was as if everything came to a head at the commencement of the Christmas break. Mr. Jones announced to a very sad class, that he was moving on to another school back in the south of England. There was no doubt that every boy would miss him and they would all be sorry to see him go, the time spent in his care had been an extremely happy one, a time never to be forgotten.

Laurie was informed at the same time that he was to be transferred to Hillocks School for the beginning of the next term. The last day at Priestly Road was one of mixed emotions and happy memories for both boys and teachers alike. Mr. Jones class spent the whole morning on the sports field playing football and rounders. When lunch break came it started off quietly but developed into a party with plenty of jokes and singing.

The crowning moment of the day came, when to the surprise of everyone, a Scottish Piper came into the classroom playing his Bagpipes, the noise was deafening, and coupled with the cheering from the boys, it made for one hilarious occasion and a fitting end to a wonderful day. After all the fun came the sad farewells. The parting of Laurie from Mr. Jones was a strange moment! As they shook hands both were close to tears, it was obvious that a strong bond of friendship had grown up between them. Laurie lacked the words in his limited vocabulary to express the feelings in his heart, but the teacher understood. He gripped Laurie's hands for several seconds, then turned and walked away without looking back, it would be a long time to the day their paths crossed again.

CHAPTER SEVEN

Hardwick Street, the first school Laurie attended in Sutton In Ashfield, stood on the west side of town, the second, Priestly Road was to the north, Hillocks lay on the very eastern end of civilization. Being on the outskirts of the main town, gave this area a very different character for various reasons. True, there were two broken down old cotton mills but these were screened from view by thick clumps of bushes. They were almost invisible from the road. Once past these, it was open country for miles and in summer ideal for long walks.

There was something which intrigued Laurie more than anything else, he had never seen anything like it before. Row upon row of gypsy caravans lined one side of the road which led out of town and into the country, while on the opposite side stood a small ordinary residential estate. It was a very odd mixture, the two extremes clashed.

Laurie no longer had a two mile walk to school, in fact Hillocks was just across the road from Grover Street where he now lived with his family. A quick one hundred yard sprint across what could have been called the Village Green and he was inside the school gates. First impressions of this part of town made one think it had been built in another century, like an outcast village.

A large triangle of grass dominated the centre. Two sides of the triangle were similar and there were some houses which had obviously been in existence for many years, but dotted in between (as if by some mistake) were six quaint little shops, the butcher, the baker, the candle stick maker. Capable of supplying every need of the people who lived close by. The third side was dominated by the school itself, which appeared comparatively modern, completely out of character with the old mills which stood dark and menacing, slightly to one side and at the back. Even Grover Street, where Laurie now lived was anything but ordinary. At the top end a mixture of old wood and scrap yards, then four small terraced houses on either side, while the bottom half was taken up with more Gypsy caravans, once again a strange combination.

As Laurie's life was about to be divided into two separate parts, now is perhaps the best time to explain his whole family background.

Wal and Floss, Laurie's mother and father, had seven children. The two eldest boys, Raymond and Bramwell were in the Royal Navy. The third, Norman Henry was already on the Canal Barges with Father. Doreen Mary number four, who had now left school and started work. Peter was number five, who was now about to leave school and also join Father on the Barges. Laurie was number six and Elizabeth the baby was number seven.

Peter was inclined to be a bit of a rebel but more about that later. During the holiday break, Laurie was allowed to spend a week on the Canal with Father, he had not known what to expect but this exciting new way of life opened up the door to adventures beyond his wildest dreams. He was really beginning to savour the true joy of living.

CHAPTER EIGHT

On his return after the holiday Laurie once more had to adjust to a different environment, much worse, another school and teacher. He arrived at Hillocks on Monday morning after the Christmas break. Laurie was now growing stronger and more sturdy with every day. He prepared to meet his new teacher but with less fear and trepidation than on previous occasions. He had much more confidence in himself now, there were at least some subjects he enjoyed and on mental arithmetic, he absolutely thrived. Once again another little shock awaited him. After assembly the boys were graded and directed to their classes. Laurie entered the room all unsuspecting and froze instantly, sitting at the desk was his old enemy, Mrs. Clark - Laurie was shattered. The recognition was immediate, her eyes never left his face as she directed him towards a seat only four feet from her desk. His heart pounding, he waited. After the register had been called, the inevitable procedure was carried out. Reading books were passed round the class, Laurie was resigned to whatever fate had in store. True to prediction the order came "Gilson come and read." Laurie reluctantly slid out from behind his desk and facing the class commenced to read. He really did try hard. Mrs. Clark listened, letting him continue for a while. He was still well behind his reading age but at least he had made some progress. She stopped him. "A little better, but not good enough" she snapped, "You are still far too lazy." Laurie returned to his seat content that at least he had avoided the cane this time. He decided that he must stay clear of Mrs. Clark at all costs.

At break time Laurie wandered round the playground, so far as he could see none of his former friends were at the school. It was then he noticed a boy about his own age sitting alone, He sat down at his side. Laurie only had time to learn that his name was Mike and that they were classmates, when the bell clanged.

On their return to class each boy found on his desk an arithmetic test paper. Addition and subtraction, ten sums in all.

"You have thirty minutes to complete," said Mrs. Clark. "Carry on." It took Laurie just six minutes to complete the test, he put down his pen and glanced round the room, looking for the boy named Mike. The sharp voice of Mrs. Clark cracked out across the room "Gilson, what do you think you are doing boy, day dreaming again?" "No Miss, I have finished," said Laurie. "Rubbish," retorted the teacher, "bring your paper to me." Mrs. Clark stared at the paper in astonished silence, it was untidy, but every sum was correct. She was speechless. Just for once Laurie had the pleasure of seeing Mrs. Clark lost for words. The pleasure was short lived. On the other side of the classroom there was a disturbance and then a terrible scream.

The boy called Mike was frothing at the mouth and throwing his body backwards and forwards across the desk. Laurie had no idea what it was all about. He didn't understand that Mike had what was called fits and if he had known, would not have understood, all he wanted to do was help him.

Quickly crossing the room he sat down beside Mike, put his arm round his shoulders and held him tight until the shaking and sobbing ceased. Mrs. Clark looked on in amazement. Mike had suffered from fits all his life but she had been warned to keep clear until they passed - she was beginning to see Laurie Gilson in a different light.

Before Laurie arrived at Hillocks, Mike Stevens had a double desk to himself, nobody else wished to sit with him. The two boys spent so much time together at playtime and in lunch breaks, that eventually they asked Mrs. Clark if Laurie could change his seat to be near Mike. The teacher agreed after consulting the Headmaster, who, on hearing about the incident in the classroom thought it a good idea. The two boys became school pals but it ended there, as Mike was collected and taken home each day because of his illness. Laurie was having difficulty in finding boys his own age to make friends with, the only children in the street where he lived were all girls, he did play with them occasionally but he missed the rougher type of game on which he thrived. One girl in particular named Janet, who was about a year older than Laurie, and also had very nice parents, would call him rude names and run away. Of course this was an invitation to chase her and Laurie would always oblige. Then one day he pursued her as far as the back door of the house in which she lived, slamming the door behind her. Just for the fun of it he hammered on the window, He failed to notice her father, who, joining in the fun, leaned out of an upstairs window and tipped a cup of cold water over Laurie's head.

It all came to an abrupt end when Laurie's fist smashed through the window. His mother was not very pleased.

CHAPTER NINE

Not too far away from Hillocks school, there was a lovely wooded area which surrounded a large lake, Known as 'Sheepwash,' it was a favourite spot for children to play. Here Laurie first met Frank and Dennis, They were much older and well into their thirteenth year, Laurie was to find out later that they were not the choicest friends to have. Frank and Dennis always seemed to be in trouble and had bad reputations. Some of their activities were, to say the least, a bit dubious, although Laurie was unaware of this at the time and quite happy to tag along when invited.

In the days that followed most of the time they spent climbing trees and splashing round the edges of the lake, Laurie soon realized that the two older boys would go into shops and while one kept the owner busy, the other would steal goods off the counter. This worried Laurie it was against everything he had been taught. He played games and went exploring with the boys for several weeks, Frank, who was obviously the leader would often pull Dennis to one side and whisper things not meant for Laurie's ears. They would talk about girls in a nasty way and when these things happened he kept clear of them.

The relationship came to an unexpected end. Frank decided that it would be a good bit of fun to have a look at the old cotton mills again, they had been whispering and Laurie knew that something was going to happen, even so, he could never have imagined what.

They had climbed over a low wall and were about to enter

the bushes that screened the old mills from the foot-path. Frank told Laurie to wait for them on the other side of the bushes, they would be with him in a minute. Laurie did as he was told but hoped that they would hurry, school had finished half an hour ago and his mother would be looking for him. He had already decided to part company with Frank and Dennis and wondered what they could be up to now.

Suddenly there was a crashing sound as someone came through the bushes, Laurie thought he heard a scream. Frank and Dennis appeared half carrying, half dragging a young girl. She had long fair hair and was struggling violently. Laurie watched horrified as Frank pulled the girl's clothes up over her head stifling her cries, while Dennis stripped the rest of her body naked.

Laurie sat petrified, it was the first time he had seen a young woman's body completely exposed in all its beauty. Just in that first few moments, it was as if Laurie had been turned into stone, his mouth and throat had dried up, he was unable to make a sound. The girl had almost given up the struggle, her sobbing was muffled by the clothes Frank held over her face, whilst Dennis sitting on her legs, had stripped off his trousers. It was only when Dennis started to force the girl's legs apart that Laurie fully realized their intentions. Something inside him snapped. He was no hero but fear was forgotten, he just went crazy, throwing himself at Frank, he butted him in the chest knocking the wind out of him and taking him off the girl's head. In that first mad charge, he had fortunately kicked Dennis in the ear, it started to bleed badly. This was a lucky break for Laurie and almost certainly saved him a good hiding. The two older boys were so taken by surprise. They had no idea where the attack had come from, they did know that they had been hit and hurt badly. Laurie had also been helped by the fact that the light had faded a little, and the bushes cast lots of shadows. Luckily the two boys panicked. Without waiting to find out who was responsible ran without looking back.

The sound of their departure faded and all was quiet. Laurie had been winded in his clash with Frank and was shaking all over. The whole terrible business had only taken a few minutes but it had left him dazed and confused. The girl was sitting propped up on one elbow, She knew that the boy, now trying to get up on his knees beside her had come to the rescue, she was so terribly upset and afraid. What was to happen now? The tears still ran down her lovely face.

Laurie was up on his feet now, collecting the girl's clothes as quick as he could. Placing them in her lap he gently squeezed her hand and sat down facing the other way. In a short while, the girl had dressed herself and was standing beside him. Laurie took her hand shyly and led her through the bushes back to the path. He asked which direction and the she pointed towards town.

The girl had still not fully recovered from her ordeal some ten minutes later, when they stopped at the gate of a neat little house. Laurie had not spoken a word all the way but now, as she opened the gate and turned to face him, Laurie, very nervous and shy stuttered, "I must run, I shall be late home," and he was gone.

For many weeks following his clash with Dennis and Frank he kept well clear of all the haunts where he knew they were most likely to be found but strange as it may sound, he never saw either of them again. Whenever he was passing the pretty little house where he had left the girl, his walking pace would slacken in the hope that she would come out and speak to him. He often laid in bed or sat on the grass opposite the school thinking of that strange evening when they first met, but never actually spoke to each other. It was possible he would never see her again.

CHAPTER TEN

The weather was gradually getting warmer as spring approached. One particular Sunday the sun was shining bright and clear. Laurie asked his mother if he could take sandwiches for lunch, and picnic over on the green - she readily agreed, preparing him some special bits and pieces.

Ten minutes later he lay back on the grass, sucking a tomato and content in his world of dreams.

He was licking his lips on the last of the tomato, his eyes closed, when a soft gentle voice asked, "May I sit down?" Laurie knew it was her even before his eyes were open. He had waited weeks to hear her voice. She sat down as he turned round and he found himself looking into that lovely face, with the long fair hair curled below the shoulders. There was now a smile, where before there had been tears.

For the first time Laurie was able to take a long look at this beautiful young woman, (for that is what she was) who he had met under such strange circumstances. He guessed that she would be all of thirteen, more than two years his senior. She was also taller than Laurie and extremely well developed. He was searching for words and felt very nervous. He had to say something so he told the truth! "I walked past your house several times, hoping that we would meet again," he managed to blurt out at last. Then she took over the conversation, her speech flowed easily. Laurie sat and listened.

"I came to say thank you," she said, and continued on without giving him chance to reply. "The evening you left so abruptly, was the day before I was due to return to boarding school but being so upset about what happened on that Sunday, I stayed at home until the Wednesday. You passed the house on the day before I went back and it was my intention to come out and speak to you but my mother advised me to wait until half-term. I would then be fully recovered from the shock and able to think straight.

My mother told me in her letters that you had passed the house on several occasions and that you were always alone." I was determined we would meet again soon.

Laurie was quite happy to listen to her speaking. Now and then he would interrupt to ask a question and soon it became a two way conversation.

Her name was Rita and her father was teaching at a school in another town some miles away. They talked easily about their likes and dislikes, about hobbies, where they were born, sport and gymnastics. The afternoon flew past, Laurie was wishing it would go on for ever. The incident which had first brought about their meeting had not been mentioned and Laurie had no wish to discuss it. He was telling Rita about his mother and the devoted way in which she had cared for him when he had been so ill. Rita could tell Laurie was very fond of his mother.

"Did you tell your mother what happened?" She asked quite suddenly, Laurie shook his head and went on to explain that it would only have worried her and he had no wish to do that.

Rita looked at Laurie, the sun was not as warm as it had been and was beginning to sink in the west. She knew she must go home soon. She wanted her mother to meet Laurie and she could tell by the questions her parents had put to her that they were concerned about the fact that she had come looking for him. It was uncanny, almost as if Laurie had the ability to read her mind. "I would like to walk home with you," he said, "but I shall have to pop home and tell my mother that I might be late. "I'll come with you," she said quickly. "Is it very far?" "No," said Laurie taking her hand quite naturally. She smiled as he almost pulled her across the road and round the corner into Grover Street.

Whatever Laurie lacked in size and education, she decided he made up for in enthusiasm. Having obtained permission but also a warning not be too late, he was soon back outside and ten minutes later they were standing at Rita's front door.

Laurie was about to say a reluctant farewell when the door opened and Mrs. Denby stood at the door smiling. She was a friendly person and really just an older version of her daughter, and although Laurie was always shy with strangers, he liked Rita's mother straight away.

Mrs. Denby gave him tea and biscuits and while she was making the tea listened as he talked to her daughter. The difference in their ages was obvious and knowing that Rita didn't make friends with just anyone, she was very curious about this lad, and just assumed it must be the unusual way they had met which was something she was still concerned about.

Mrs. Denby loved her daughter and was also very proud of her achievements. At school she had excelled herself in sport and most of her studies. If nothing else, they owed this young boy a debt of gratitude. She shuddered at the thought of what might have happened if he had not been around to intervene on that dreadful evening.

Now as she entered the room Laurie hardly noticed, he was excitedly telling Rita about his weeks holiday with his father on the Grand Union Canal, where his father evidently skippered two barges. He went on to explain that it meant his father was away from home most of the time, and the job was a special assignment to transport coal by barge from Langley Mill down to London. He explained that his family had been fishermen for generations and that after the war he would be going back to the South Coast to take his place aboard a fishing boat and spend his life at sea.

He went on to say that his Great Grandfather had been a smuggler in the old days, sailing backwards and forwards across the English Channel carrying contraband. Mrs. Denby listened closely. Either the boy was telling the truth or he was a fantastic story teller. Looking at her daughter was enough to convince her that at least one person had been captivated. The vivid picture that he was now painting of the colourful barges left no doubt in her mind that he was genuine. She herself had seen them many times.

They had all been so absorbed in the stories that no one had noticed the arrival of Mr. Denby, he had been standing unnoticed outside the door for ten minutes or more, listening. There were many questions he had intended asking this lad but listening to him speak, they no longer seemed important.

He made his presence known. Kissing his wife and daughter, he then shook hands with Laurie. "So this is our hero," he said, Laurie felt a bit apprehensive. "I shall be careful not to tangle with you," he said, laughing. "And I never fight with schoolmasters," Laurie said, "I always lose!" They all laughed. When Laurie had gone home, Mrs. Denby looked at her husband, "What do you think?" She said. "I think Laurie Gilson will one day be a fisherman and own his own boat but he will have to grow a bit first." Mrs. Denby smiled, she asked, "You know what I mean, what about this friendship?" "Well put it this way" said her husband, "I would be quite happy if he were my friend.".

Laurie went back to school the following day, more content with life than at any time since leaving his home town. He now lived with his own family, who became good friends with the Denbys. This meant that whenever Rita was home, He was allowed to visit.

The effect this had on Laurie's education was astounding. The time spent with Rita had improved his reading beyond belief. He was now taking an interest in adventure books, comics, and history. Rita persuaded him to read aloud, and she would correct his mistakes. Laurie was no longer afraid of lessons, He settled down at Hillocks School and gradually began to catch up with the rest of his class in most subjects.

He revelled in sport of any kind, and would stand kicking anything that resembled a ball, against a wall for hours on end. Time now passed quickly by and it had been planned that Laurie would spend the first week of the summer holidays at home but the following three weeks he would go with his father on the Canal barges.

CHAPTER ELEVEN

The school term came quickly to its conclusion, leaving Laurie with one sad thought - Mrs. Clark, the little grey haired teacher, who had followed him from one school after another and plagued the life out of him without mercy, left to go back south before the improvement in his reading became evident. She might never know that he could now read quite fluently.

Most of the first week's holiday was spent in the company of Rita, they had picnics, and went for long walks through the lovely countryside. They raced each other over different distances and would sit and talk for hours. Their relationship was a very deep friendship, based on the fact that they had so much in common despite the two year age gap. They were always relaxed in each others company. Rita knew she would miss Laurie in the weeks ahead when he left to join his father on the barges.

On the Saturday Laurie left for the station, the journey was part train part bus. Rita walked with him to the station. They stood waiting on the platform and as the train came into view, for the first time since they had met, she put her arms round Laurie and held him close. Laurie was flustered, that unstoppable surge of energy, which made him feel so guilty, flooded through his body and he clung to her. Just for that moment he held her tight, She squeezed him and he knew she understood.

When Laurie arrived at Langley Mill, the barges were being loaded. His father and brothers were covered in coal dust. He soon changed into his old clothes and was in the thick of it.

From this point in time, he was in another world and he had to adjust. Life on the barges was somehow separated from the rest of the world.

The coal was full of fumes and choking dust, it was almost a case of being hosed down after loading was completed. Laurie's brother Peter decided that the best way to get clean was to dive into the cut (as the Canal was called) with a bar of soap. He took off his clothes, and jumped in, stark naked! It just so happened at that time a school mistress with a class of senior girls, out on a nature study, came along the towpath, and stopped to admire the colourful barges.

They asked Laurie where the coal was being transported to, he explained that the barges were bound for London the next day, but that his brother, who was taking a swim, always stayed in the water ages. Would they like to go on the barges and have a look round.

The girls, thoroughly enjoying themselves waved to Peter, who was fuming. He had been in the water for some time, he was getting chilly and wanted to get out. Each time he went to either end of the barges, Laurie would bring the girls along to meet him and of course being naked, he had to swim away again.

The girls by this time had realized the joke that was being played on the swimmer and loved it. The situation was saved by the arrival of Laurie's father, who quickly sized up what was going on and with a broad grin on his face, took the girls on a guided tour of the engine room much to their disappointment. Peter, blue and shivering, climbed out of the water. Laurie said, "Great day for a swim!" Peter scowled and shook his fist at Laurie.

One of the most enjoyable things about being on the Canal barges with his brothers, were the jokes they were always playing on each other. Peter soon got his revenge on Laurie. That same evening before they left Langley Mill, the two of them at Peter's suggestion, went up onto the railway track where there were hundreds of trucks, some loaded, others empty and waiting to be pulled away. "If you climb up on top of the end truck Lol" Peter instructed, "you will be able to see the first bridge that we go under in the morning."

Without giving it a second thought, Laurie started to climb, and was soon up on top of the empty carriage, searching for the bridge. He was so engrossed, he failed to notice that Peter had unhooked the truck and was pushing as hard as he could.

Before Laurie realized what was happening he was travelling at speed along the track, what's more, it was too late for him to do very much about it. He had no idea at the time where he was heading, He only knew he was gaining speed every second and was considering what his chances would be if he were to make a jump for it, when there was an almighty crash. The truck had hit the buffers at the end of the track. Laurie landed in a heap at the bottom of the truck black and blue from dust and bruises. Peter had taken his revenge.

It was still dark but there was much activity on board the two barges. They were referred to as the Motor Boat and the Butty. The Motor Boat was powered by a twenty horse power diesel engine, which at the moment was chugging away contentedly. The engine itself made very little noise but the exhaust, which came out through a large black funnel, decorated by three circles of gleaming brass, made a hollow sound positively ear splitting in the silence of the night.

Ten minutes later the mooring ropes had been cast off and the Motor Boat, with father in charge, took the Butty in tow. The two older brothers each taking turn to be Skipper.

They where approaching the first bridge as daylight began to break in the eastern sky. Great care had to be taken, most of the bridges were often very low and arched, which meant that the barges were forced to stay in the centre or risk losing paint on the rough sides of the bridge wall. Having safely passed through, they were now on their way.

With each moment the light increased, showing up the trees and bushes on either side of the towpath. The paths which ran along all the canals were called towpaths because originally the barges were drawn by horses. In fact at that point in time, one horse drawn barge was still in operation.

Soon the sun came up from behind the trees showing up the countryside in all its glory. The rays of the sun, shining through different shades of green on the water, gave it a breathtaking beauty. It was indeed a wonderful sight to behold.

Now once again there was work to be done. It was all action, due to the fact that they were approaching the first lock. It appeared that the gates were closed against them, this meant that a vessel had already passed through ahead of them going in the same direction. As a result of this Peter and Laurie would have to land on the bank, take Peter's bike with them and ride on ahead

They only possessed one bike, Laurie rode on the crossbar. As you can imagine the boats made very slow progress and it was customary to put the two boys on the bank about a mile before the lock was reached. This gave ample time to prepare for the barges to enter.

On this occasion the lock was up hill, which would mean the sluices on the first gates would have to be opened. A specially made handle slipped onto the square ended gear shaft and had to be turned some fifty times in order to let the water out, it was heavy work.

The gates could then be opened to receive the oncoming barges. Once safely inside, the gates were closed and the whole operation reversed. When the lock had refilled, the opposite end gates were opened and the barges were clear to continue on their way. Sometimes there would be several locks on end and in one place, they had to pass through forty-two locks just to get to the top of one hill, it was a laborious task.

Life on the canal was great fun, there was always something happening. On several occasions Peter and Laurie riding on ahead to prepare the next lock, slipped off the towpath and fell into the water, bike as well, it was hilarious, especially when Peter received a clip round the ear from Father for being careless. Laurie would laugh and then get chased along the towpath and finish up fighting with Peter in the long grass until they had dried off.

On one particular day they were passing through a village where there were ten locks bunched together. Father told Peter to take the water butts and fill them. Now the water butts (as you may guess) were the containers in which they carried the drinking water, there were four butts and each one carried about six gallons of water, it was the usual routine to top them up at every lock keeper's cottage.

The taps always being round at the back of the building. Peter calling Laurie to help him, collected the water butts and proceeded on round the back of the cottage. When they arrived in the garden, their mouths watered at the sight of the delicious apples that hung from a whole orchard of trees. This was to much of a temptation for Peter. He told Laurie to fill two of the water butts with water, The other two he took into the orchard as quickly as he could and put about ten pounds of apples in each. He then handed Laurie the butts in which the apples were hidden, then grabbing the two that were full of water, headed back to the barges.

As they carried the butts across to the barges, Father was standing talking to the lock keeper. Father, (who was pretty observant and missed very little) remarked "Those butts don't look very full." He was referring to the two that Laurie was carrying. "It's alright Dad" said Peter, "we are going to top up all the pots and then refill them."

At that moment Laurie unfortunately tripped (possibly because he felt guilty) and the result was that suddenly the ground was strewn with apples. There was a deathly silence, Then Peter began to run, but not fast enough, Father caught him before he had gone fifty yards along the towpath, and as a result of the good hiding his bottom was sore for several days.

CHAPTER TWELVE

Although it was an inland waterway, there were many dangerous obstacles to overcome on the long journey down from London, sometimes there would be a lack of water in the canal, at other times, it would be in flood. One of the most difficult and dangerous tasks was crossing the River Trent when in flood. The long narrow barges with such small engines, had to wait for the right moment to cross from one side to the other, which they were forced to do in order to get to London, or they could be in big trouble. Looking back on the whole structure of the canal systems, the locks, the dependence on the rain and natural water supply, the dangerously underpowered barges, the only definite thing to be said in its favour was that it provided cheap transport but it was very slow.

Laurie got his first look at Trent Lock at about six o'clock on a fine summer's evening. This was the gateway to this most famous river that runs through the heart of England. The ropes were made fast to the posts which had been firmly set in concrete, the barges moored to these, would lay safe and secure for the night.

Peter and Laurie were now free to explore, Father had decided that the dangerous crossing would be better left until the following morning. The river was running quite high and there was a fast flow of tide.

Left to their own devices (but with a warning not to get into trouble) the two boys set off. Peter had been here before so he knew several places of interest to make for. In a small creek not far from the Lock, they came across another pair of barges that were laid up for painting. There were several children playing in the field close by.

These were real bargees, people who had spent their whole lives on the canal. They could neither read or write, the only time they went to school was at times like this, when the boats had to refit, but then it would only be for a few days. They were always friendly people and never appeared hurried, they might not be educated but they were skilful in many other ways. Their barges, (being home, and all they possessed) were always spotlessly clean. The cabins in which they ate and slept were all decorated with copper and brass. Everything that could be painted a bright colour to increase smartness, was painted, but always in good taste, they were more house-proud than any people that lived on land.

As Peter and Laurie approached, the children came to meet them. Two boys, so alike that they might have been twins were about thirteen years of age, then a girl somewhat older possibly sixteen, then two much younger children less than five, these were obviously in the older girls care.

The two boys had catapults in their hands but they were all smiles as they dashed across the field to greet the newcomers. Names and ages were soon exchanged. Then for some considerable time they sat talking.

Laurie was interested in the two boys and the catapults. Alf and Gery showed him how skilled they were, with what Father would have called 'those dangerous weapons' Peter was more interested in talking to Joan, who was a pretty girl with raven black hair which hung in long ringlets down her back. He had never seen hair so long and shiny. He quite obviously wished that the stop at Trent Lock could have been a much longer one but it wasn't to be and all the wishing in the world could not alter the fact that it was now getting dusk. They must soon take leave of these new found friends and head back for their own barges, as it was going to be an early start tomorrow morning.

This was the way of life on the canal, people would meet and make friends, then part and not meet again for weeks, months, even years, perhaps never and this was to be the case with Peter and Joan. As they all parted, Joan kissed Peter on the cheek, turned and walked quickly away without looking back. They never met again.

As the two boys made their way to the lock, Peter was very quiet, he walked just in front of Laurie and it was now almost dark. They had crossed some *Mars*hy ground in daylight earlier in the evening.

Without really noticing it they must have jumped across many ditches which were no longer visible in the dark. They were taken completely by surprise! One moment dry, the next up to the knees in mud and splashed all over with large black blobs of mud. They crawled out of the mud, fighting each other, both laughing. The mood had passed.

Living accommodation on the barges was very restricted and one of the most difficult things was having a good bath. As one can imagine, with all the coal dust flying about it became something of an occasion to be completely submerged in really hot soapy water. It became a sort of celebration but not too often possible.

When the boys arrived back from their outing, all covered in mud,they had a problem as to how they could get themselves clean without waking Father and Henry. It would not be possible in the cabin where they were almost certain to be asleep, plus the fact that Peter was not at all happy that Father should know how late they were getting back. He knew that as the eldest, he would be the one to be carpeted. Finally, after some discussion,they came to the conclusion that the cut (as the canal was known) was the only answer.

Stripping off they jumped into the cold water taking their clothes with them. Fortunately, the water was not too cold (the sun having shone all day) and only having a shirt and shorts to wash, The task was soon accomplished. After wringing out the clothes they crept back aboard but the hardest part was yet to come. All four slept in the same cabin. The sleeping accommodation was in some ways pretty unique if somewhat primitive. Every inch of space had to be utilised and serve more than one purpose, each unit built into the side of the barge served as a wardrobe, food cupboard, linen shelf or whatever one wished to use it for. When closed, these units held all the domestic gear, footwear, clothes, and all else that completes any normal household leaving the floor area clear and the cabin neat and tidy. Each folding door, drop-down hatch, hinged panel, when open became a seat, dining room table, bedstead or mirror. No space or piece of woodwork went to waste, everything in that cosy little cabin was essential.

The problem the boys had, was to get into bed unheard. This all sounds simple enough, except that they slept below Father and Henry, who slept on a five foot drop hatch lowered across the cabin which locked into a seat bench on the opposite side. This left a twenty four inch gap above the floor, which was where Peter and Laurie slept. As one can imagine, the cavity into which Peter and Laurie had to slide was not very big but the operation was accomplished without hindrance from above. Soon they were both sound asleep.

Early next morning the alarm bell sounded out loud and clear that a new day awaited. Normally Father would be first up, put the kettle on then proceed up through the cabin hatch to study the weather. What the boys were unaware of was that Father had turned in first the previous night and had slept on the inside berth. It was Henry who was now on deck, and Father who still lay in the bunk, contemplating the day ahead. Peter and Laurie constantly played pranks on brother Henry but one was about to misfire. Stuck in the bulkhead they kept a long needle which they had used on several occasions when Henry overslept. Not hearing any movement from above, out came the needle. It was pushed gently up through the bunk until it made contact. The response was a roar from Father which appeared to shake the cabin. In a split second the two boys slid out and made for the escape hatch but fast as they were, it was not fast enough. Grabbed unceremoniously from behind, both paid the penalty with a good thrashing - not the best of ways to start a new day.

CHAPTER THIRTEEN

At day-light the lock was made ready for them to enter, The gates closed behind them as soon as the boats were inside. Gears groaned and the great sluices at the other end of the lock opened, releasing hundreds of tons of water, thus lowering barges and men down to the level of the mighty River Trent.

It was an awesome sight to behold as the barges (like tiny corks) motored out of the lock. With such a strong tide running it appeared at first they would be swept away. Father was prepared for the mighty rush of water and even before they were out of the lock, had brought the barges almost head into the tide. They had already battened down the hatch covers, which was just as well. Water lapped over the topsides and spray flew everywhere. The fresh wind, blowing in an opposite direction, against the tide, made it a very choppy crossing. It took much concentration and careful handling to navigate crab fashion from one side of the river to the other. Laurie kept looking over his shoulder to a point down stream, for there, roughly a half mile away. Stretching from one side of the Trent to the other, stood a weir, blocking the river like a dam.

It had in the past proved to be the graveyard of many boats when the river was in flood, fortunately, all went well! The barges entered the smooth water of the canal on the other side without mishap, much to Father's relief. Crossing the Trent always caused some concern.

The next part of their journey although enjoyable proved

uneventful. Maintenance on the boats amounted to washing, scrubbing, and generally keeping everything clean and tidy. Laurie would spend much of his time running along the towpath collecting souvenirs to take back to his mother and sister. Whenever a lock had to be opened, out came the old bike and Peter would jump off at a convenient spot, the two of them dashing on ahead in order to prepare for the arrival of the barges. Sometimes a pair of boats going in the opposite direction might be using the lock but if this was the case it caused little or no delay and in some cases could mean that miles of canal could be navigated without opening one single lock

It turned out to be a good run down to Loughborough where sometimes the barges would unload, but not this time, they needed some stores. Apart from this, Father had made a friend of the crane driver, often stopping for a good chin-wag and passing a pleasant evening together.

Tom, the crane driver, owned an old steam roller, it was his pride and joy. He loved to tell stories of how, in the old days, it was his steam roller that made many of the main roads in the town. He boasted that, if needed, the old girl, as he called her, would run good as ever.

Now this was something old Tom ought not to have said - well at least not within hearing range of the boys. The two men, almost into their fifties, had led such varied lives, they would talk endlessly about their differing experiences, and were quite happy to do so in between many cups of tea. Awareness of the present, diverted for the moment, they basked in the glory of another era. This did not apply to Laurie and Peter. Old Tom's tales of adventure in the steamroller roused their curiosity, they had to know more about this enormous black creature. Although it stood alone in the corner, away from all other activity, this old powerful beast from another age had lost none of its former beauty. Tom made sure the old girl was kept greased and painted. 'Good as new,' was how he described her. The boys first carried out a complete examination, they climbed into the steering house pulling the levers, turning wheels, opening and closing valves.

It was all good fun! They were content with this for best part of an hour. It was while the furnace door was open that the first seed of an idea was born. Looking into the pitch dark void, they were unable to see a thing. It just so happened that Laurie had a box of matches in his pocket. Taking a match from the box, he struck it as he leaned forward into the furnace. The light flared, showing a pile of oily rages - they had discovered the place where Tom kept all his old cleaning rags. He must have been storing them there for years. What happened next may have been an accident, but Laurie dropped the match when it started to burn his fingers. Still alight, it fell into the rags - the outcome was frightening. The rags exploded into flame, they were so fierce both boys jumped back in alarm. Long tongues of flame leapt out of the furnace into the steering house. Peter slammed the furnace door shut and turned the handle to the point that indicated 'locked'. If the boys were surprised at developments inside the steering house, it was nothing to compare with the scene outside. Thick black smoke belched from the eight foot high chimney, it rose in great stinking clouds above the town. Someone phoned the fire brigade, while back in the steamroller the boys could hear (to begin with) quiet hissing sounds, rapidly growing louder. Soon steam started to pour from the cab out of which Peter and Laurie, choking for breath, jumped for their lives. The clang of the fire engine bell brought Father and old Tom, white faced and running from the barges. People appeared from all directions. It was chaos. Looking back to that day it was hysterically funny, but this was one time that Laurie and Peter decided it would not be wise to stay to enjoy it. After the catastrophe at Loughborough with old Tom's steamroller, the boys felt that under the circumstances it would be in their best interest to keep a low profile for some time. They continued to torment Henry whenever the chance was offered, but kept clear of Father as much as possible.

CHAPTER FOURTEEN

At the next large town on the route down the canal, they stayed a full twenty four hours. As Laurie found out later, it was a city not a town, called Leicester. It was a city of some considerable size, quite apart from the endless rows of warehouses, which were stocked with every kind of commodity you could imagine. One thing in particular stood out in his mind, that was the very wide, busy main road it was extremely dangerous for pedestrians.

It was nothing unusual to stand at the roadside for long periods of time attempting to dodge through the continuous traffic. Laurie had never seen anything like it, the cars, trams and lorries heading for the canal docks seemed endless. There were plenty of interesting things for Peter and Laurie to do, they managed to scrounge a whole hundredweight bag of caster sugar from one of the unloading barges. The bags were lifted from the vessel's hold in packs of ten. Often a bag suffered damage if it touched the side of the hold on the way up. Although directions to the crane driver were being given all the time from the deck, accidents happened. If sugar spewed from the bag, it was laid to one side. This was exactly what happened, the boys were there at just the right time. A badly torn bag was discarded, it had already lost several pounds of sugar and they were attempting to block the large hole with paper, but there were also lots of smaller holes. The dockers watched their efforts to stop the leaks for some time. It caused considerable amusement, but eventually the ganger came along and seeing the state of the bag told Peter and

Laurie they could take it away. The lads needed no second bidding dragging the sugar behind them, they made off to the barges with their much treasured prize. It took a long time to convince Father that it had not been stolen. He declined the offer of going back to the unloading bay to confirm the boys story just in case. He had to admit the sugar was very welcome and this huge supply would last for weeks.

The following morning at first light they were once more on their way. As the sun came up it was obviously going to be another beautiful day. They chugged away through the lovely countryside, all the wonders of nature unfolded before them. Laurie, (dressed only in shorts,) lay on top of the Butty boat's cabin, the air was so fresh and clean, the sun warm on his back, it was good to be alive. The smell of the trees and flowers wafted across the water of the canal, the many different types of birds would fly from one bank to the other, gliding gently across with wings outstretched, showing off the glorious colours of their plumage, it was almost as if they were aware that Laurie was watching, and had put on a special display.

Along both sides of the canal grew large patches of water lilies, thousands upon thousands of enormous white blooms. They sensed the approach of the barges, or could feel the vibrations in the water, for by the time Laurie was close enough to look directly down on them, they had folded their petals and disappeared beneath the water. Sometimes, on either side, the water lay thick with giant bulrushes and the moorhens dashed in and out tending their nests. Often the boys collected the eggs, they were nice to eat and in plentiful supply, small but tasty. All these wonderful experiences were just part of a normal day in the life of the canal.

There was often the unusual as well. On one particular day, as the barges were about to swing round a large half circle bend, Henry, who was steering the Butty at the time, noticed that on the right hand bank (which was the side they would swing into) branches of delicious looking plums hung well out over the water. It was a simple matter to put the helm hard over, and bring the cabin of the Butty close in underneath the overhanging fruit. The progress of the barges being so slow, Henry had ample time to reach up and slide his hands down three branches separately. Laurie, standing in the cabin hatch, held the bottom of the branch in place over the hatch and down in the cabin it rained plums. It was a very good haul.

Meanwhile Father, who skippered the motor barge in front, was looking back, shaking his fist at Henry, he had witnessed everything that had taken place. In his code of behaviour this was stealing. There was sure to be retribution later on, when they stopped for the night. At the moment the three boys sat on board the Butty boat content that they were safe for the time being and happily sucking the juicy plums, which had been equally shared out. With a bit of luck, Father might have cooled down by the end of the long day ahead. Having contact with, and spending so much time in the company of his brothers, quickly increased Laurie's general knowledge.

Much of the mystery about life and death, plus most of the important things that occurred in between, would be quite openly discussed in his presence. He now understood what made the blood race through his veins and stiffen his body, and the outcome, if followed through to its ultimate conclusion. He had yet four months to reach his eleventh birthday, but even so endured all the pleasure, pain and guilt of growing older. Laurie thoroughly enjoyed the journey down to London and fully realized what a great opportunity (which by an accumulation of circumstances) had come his way, he knew he was one in a million, and in spite of a very poor start in life, some one or some thing was looking after him. He had little education, but great ambition. There were many further exciting adventures and comical moments to be experienced before the barges reached their destination at Limehouse.

Laurie never did understand why, but Peter and Henry always appeared to be at each other's throats. Hardly a day went past without a stand up fight or a set to of some sort.

Peter usually instigated the problem, but also suffered the most good hidings. On this particular occasion, once again it was Peter who started the trouble, but Henry that finished up getting the hiding. Poor Father must have wondered what to do with them at times, he had to act as mediator, judge and hangman! The barges always received top priority treatment. Just the suggestion of damage to either vessel, where Father was concerned, and the ground shook.

It just so happened that one place where they moored over night lay within a few yards of a sand and gravel company. As one would expect, there was an abundance of stones everywhere. Towards evening Henry went for his usual stroll. Peter and Laurie decided to inspect the sand quarry. All three were returning to the barges at the same time, but from different directions. Henry had crossed a bridge which was some thirty yards west of the boats, walking east. The other two boys stayed on the same side as the boats were moored but moved also in an easterly direction. Now, as they returned it was on opposite banks. Peter as usual making rude remarks, to which Henry was not slow to respond. Peter's next move worried Laurie a bit, he started to pelt Henry with stones. Once more Henry responded, but unfortunately for him, there were only large stones on his side of the canal, and even worse, Peter and Laurie were sheltering behind the barges.

There was a loud crash as a stone hit the Butty boat cabin, a bull's-eye, smack on the spot where Father's head lay on his bunk. He came up out of the cabin with the speed of light, roaring like a lion.

Poor Henry was caught red handed, he had another stone in his hand ready to throw, as Father appeared on deck looking straight across at him.

What happened next was pure comedy (although Henry might not have agreed.) He dropped the stone and started to run away up the hill and over a stile towards the town. Father jumped from the Butty onto the Motor boat and from there to the towpath to take up the chase. In the half light and his great haste he caught his foot on one of the mooring ropes and fell headfirst in about six inches of water. Undaunted he jumped up, took up the chase once again, over the hill he went, almost leapfrogged the stile and disappeared in hot pursuit of Henry. Peter and Laurie sat on the canal bank, doubled up with laughter. They might as well laugh now, it would probably be a much different story when Father returned from the chase. They decided that the wisest move for them would be to get turned in, discretion was the better part of valour, hopefully Father would cool down before morning. They went to sleep smiling at the thought of Henry heading for the hills with Father in hot pursuit.

Readers of these escapades may have begun to form the opinion that Laurie's father must have been always on the warpath or indeed some kind of tyrant. This was far from true, he tempered justice with mercy and could always see the funny side of a situation, but would laugh quietly to himself when left alone. He was an excellent cook, his puddings were a meal in themselves. Roly-poly pudding, bread, or bread and butter puddings, plus egg custard, were his speciality. However hard the work or how difficult the task, he never spared himself in his efforts to ensure that his family were always well fed and cared for. He was a strict, but good father. One stretch of river, through which the barges had to pass, was called 'The Twenty Mile Reach'. It was without locks, bridges, or anything else for that matter to impede the progress of the two narrow boats on their way to London. Father considered the clear passage ahead as being safe water and decided it time that Henry take charge of the Motor boat, leaving Peter to skipper the Butty. It would be good for them to take full responsibility. This would also give him time to carry out several repair jobs which badly needed attention.

All went well and they made good time, there was very little tide so Henry kept to the centre of the river, staying clear of any trouble that might be lurking close in along either bank. Just from looking at the banks, Laurie could tell that the water was very high, although not in flood. He was talking to Peter about this and at the same time letting his glance wander, when he thought he saw something swimming between the barges and river bank. He was on the point of bringing this to Peter's attention, when he saw another, and another Peter had also seen them. They were rats! Dozens and dozens of rats, some dead, some swimming for their lives. There were large rats, small rats, all colours, shapes and sizes. Peter explained to Laurie that when the river was very high, it sometimes rose above the holes in the river bank where the rats lived. Many thousands would be killed, but those that survived would return the nests. It was Nature's way of sorting out the weak and keeping numbers down. Laurie stood watching sadly, as hundreds of bloated bodies passed by. Suddenly there was a much larger object coming towards them, it came so close alongside, they could have reached out and touched it.

At first sight Laurie thought it was a small boat, but Peter who had seen it all before, recognized instantly that it was a dead sheep, its stomach bloated out of all proportion. Laurie felt rather upset seeing so many dead animals. He kept rabbits at home and even knew boys at school who had showed him their tame rats.

Once more something else distracted his attention, on the left bank, just ahead of them, several men carrying ropes were standing at the water's edge. At first it appeared, from a distance, that they were just throwing ropes into the water, then pulling them back again. As the barges came closer, Laurie could see that there was something in the water and the men were attempting to lasso it. Henry slowed the engine in the Motor boat, reducing their speed to a crawl, the barges now were hardly moving ahead. On hearing the engine decrease revolutions, Father quickly arrived on deck. He spoke first to Henry, then hurried forward to the bows of the barge, away from the noise of the engine exhaust, in order to speak without shouting. It turned out that a cow had slid down the bank into the water and was unable to get out. The farmers were attempting to get a noose over its head, the poor creature was going crazy, and obviously in real trouble. Father gave orders for Henry to edge the barge in as close to the bank as possible, at the same time asking the farmers if they would like some assistance, which they gratefully accepted. Father told the farmers to throw him a coil of rope which they did without question, the barge was now almost over the top of the cow, and as the barge was loaded, only some three feet above. It was not too difficult a task getting the noose over the animal's head. Father was successful at his second attempt, pulling it tight, he threw the loose end ashore to the farmers, who began to pull. Pulling with all their might, sure enough the cow began to move in and up the bank, sensing that it was being rescued from certain death, the animal now began to help itself. It just so happened that at this particular spot, the bank was not too steep. Soon the cow stood on the top of the canal bank surrounded by the smiling farmers who happily shouted their thanks to Father for his help. "Anytime," he replied, turning to give Henry instructions to get the barges underway again, and as they slowly gathered speed, stood waving goodbye to each other, it was good to be on friendly terms with the farmers, in fact it made a nice change.

CHAPTER FIFTEEN

Although he had no way of knowing it, any pleasant feeling about being on good terms with the farmers was soon to disappear. As has already been stated before, people that worked and lived on barges took much pride in the little narrow vessels, apart from just being smart. Laurie supposed that the objective was to be the best. One thing that has not been mentioned, is the fact that both of the barges had names. The Motor boat carried the illustrious name of *Orpheus*, the Butty boat was *Mars*. Laurie always thought it should have been the other way round because *Mars* was the smarter of the two.

The boats always carried decorative funnels, on the motor boat it was for the engine exhaust, on the Butty boat it served as the chimney for a cooking stove installed in the tiny cabin. It took all soot and smoke clear of the pretty little vessel, keeping her neat and tidy, but the funnel on *Mars* had seen better days and Peter had been keeping his eyes open for a new one. All the boats were standard built, so the fittings were also standard. This meant that any funnel fitted any boat. Just a few miles past the incident with cow catching was berthed an extremely well kept non-working barge that was owned by a wealthy farmer. Peter had admired her brass banded funnel once before when the boats had passed this way. He failed to understand why such a beautiful piece of equipment should stand unused for such long periods of time.

They were now approaching the place where the barge usually berthed, sure enough she was still there. Father had gone back down below. Peter signalled to Henry that he wanted a closer look. Henry, who took a keen interest in other vessels, was also curious about this one, so obligingly he steered almost alongside. To be able and capable of visualizing what happened in the next few moments, one has to remember that the barge only travel at walking speed, otherwise it would have been impossible, even so it was quite unbelievable. Peter explained his plan. He would leave the steering of the Butty to Laurie, they had to be extremely careful. If the barges suffered any damage, there would be hell to pay. Laurie was to steer the bow of the Butty as close to the other barges stern as possible, without touching. Peter had already unshipped the Butty's funnel in preparation for the assault. It was his intention to swap funnels with the farmer's barge. They were coming up abreast of the other vessel now. Laurie edged closer. Peter stood on the bow of the Butty, he signalled to Laurie "A little more helm." The two barges were almost touching. Peter balanced on the bow, firmly holding the Butty funnel in both arms, leapt for the stern of the other barge, landing safely on the deck, he then made a dash for the cabin. Quickly whipping off the beautiful brass banded funnel, he replaced it with the old one from the Butty, the plan was working like a dream.

Suddenly there was a loud bang, followed by a lot of shouting. The owner had witnessed the whole event and was now running across a field, shotgun in hand. Peter had taken about five paces along the deck and was preparing to re-board the Butty when the shot rang out. Quickly summing up the situation, he turned, raced back to the cabin, changed the funnels back again to their rightful place, then once more set off along the deck at speed, the old funnel tucked firmly under one arm. It was going to be touch and go now as to whether he would have time to get back on the Butty before she went past. The stern, with Laurie at the helm, was now almost up to the bow of the farmer's barge. Laurie had the stern in so tight that he could reach out and touch the side of the other vessel. The crucial moment had come. There was now a gap between the two barges of some twelve inches, but it was getting wider. Peter still had several paces to come before he could make the jump. Laurie's heart was thumping, there was nothing he could do. Slow as the barges moved, it was going to be just a bit too much. Unbelievably it was Henry who saved the situation. He had watched the whole stunt in amazement, but realizing what was about to happen, he slowed the barges down by reducing the engine revs. This gave Peter a couple of valuable seconds, unfortunately the reduction of revs also brought Father back up on deck, just in time to see Peter make his famous leap. He landed on top of Laurie and both disappeared in a messy heap, funnel on top. Both boys came up unhurt and smiling, but the smile was soon wiped away when they saw Father, standing on the deck with Henry, giving that familiar shake of his fist and running along the canal bank, the farmer with his shotgun.

Time spent on the canal passed quickly, the long summer days seemed to get shorter as the distance to London grew less. It was nothing unusual for the barges to be underway as much as eighteen hours in one day. On more than one occasion, if the weather was good, with a bright moon, they would continue on through right round the clock. It was always better to be ahead of time, rather than behind. Delays occurred often, sometimes a lock might need major repairs, or where some erosion had taken place, the collapse of a canal bank that would have to be dug out and made good. These were but a few of the many problems that could bring to a halt the long, slow winding journey South.

CHAPTER SIXTEEN

The *Orpheus* and *Mars*, with Laurie on board, had the misfortune to meet up with the last horse-drawn barge still in operation. It was in some ways a novel experience and Laurie thoroughly enjoyed it, but it did hold them up for some time. Normally the canal would either run straight on through the middle of a town, or just bypass it going all the way round the outside, but this one was different. The town was built on a hill, a two mile long tunnel through the middle of the hill, carried the canal. When the *Orpheus* and *Mars* reached the northern entrance, the horse-drawn barge was just entering the southern end. This caused a long delay. Looking back over the many years, Laurie thought that the method used by the bargees to get through the tunnel was, to say the least, ridiculous, almost comical, but effective, so long as you had a good strong pair of legs, plus a back that was capable of many hours hard graft. The whole family would lay on their backs on top of the cabin and push with their feet on the roof of the tunnel. The harder you pushed, the faster the barge travelled through the water.

Over the years Laurie had forgotten how long it took for them to come through, but the horse, which came over the hill and round the streets of the town, enjoyed a good feed and well earned rest. Laurie was thinking to himself, 'If horses have thoughts, this one must have considered it was a good time to be a horse.' When eventually the barge emerged from the tunnel, they pulled alongside, greetings were exchanged over the proverbial cup of tea, and Laurie sat listening while his Father swapped yarns with these people, who were the original Bargee Gypsy, his father was curious as to why they never modernized and converted to engines. He (as a fisherman) had seen the change from sail to engine propulsion, and the difference it made, but the Bargees answer was simple, it only made life go faster, and they were quite happy with their way of life. Laurie's father agreed that was the most important thing. They shook hands and went their separate ways.

For an ordinary human being, living in modern times, this way of life would seem absolutely ridiculous, but Laurie had just caught the end of an era which had been left behind. It was the end of a generation of people that enjoyed a contented way of life, dependent on muscle, the will to survive and be completely happy. Time had passed them by. Laurie remembered their passage through the tunnel, as a weird but uneventful experience. The darkness and slimy dripping walls gave him the impression that he was in some kind of dungeon.

The only respite from this horrible feeling was the enormous air vents, which measured roughly twenty feet across and reached vertically for the surface, hundreds of feet above. Water poured down the walls off the vents, drenching all that passed underneath. It was a considerable fete of engineering, but he was not sorry when they emerged into the bright sunshine at the other end. Laurie turned to look at the gigantic mass of rock underneath which the barges had passed. It must have amounted to millions of tons. He wondered how long it had taken to build and who was the engineer with so much courage to attempt such a mammoth task, with so little machinery. The tunnel appeared to be very old and yet there were no visible signs of recent repair, the brickwork was obviously original and each piece fitted in like a jigsaw puzzle. One could only stand back and admire such an accomplishment.

The green hills above and on either side reminded Laurie of the town in Nottinghamshire which (for the time being) he had recognised as home. He laid back on top of the Butty boat cabin top and wondered how his mother and sisters were getting on. He still missed them, not in the same way as when he was younger, not as much as he did on that horrible day, the day when he first left the South of England, just the thought of it made him shiver. With the warm sunshine blazing down on him, he dreamed about the long walks in the beautiful countryside with Rita. He was almost asleep as he wondered what she would be doing at this moment, had she forgotten him? He was so much younger than her, just a mere boy in comparison to a young woman. With that in his mind, he fell asleep.

CHAPTER SEVENTEEN

As Laurie stood on the stern of the Butty boat, *Mars*, there was no doubt in his mind whatsoever that they had nearly reached their destination, the sky was alive with searchlights. Father allowed him to stay up and enjoy the fantastic display but with strict orders not to leave the barges. They were still fifteen miles from Limehouse to the Dock where the coal was to be unloaded. The air raid warnings had gradually increased in number as they approached London, and were now virtually continuous, especially at night. As Laurie gazed in wonder at the illuminated heavens just that short distance away, the rapid thump of guns made the whole affair like a Guy Fawkes night gone mad. Peter explained to Laurie that the louder, heavier thuds were bombs, smashing buildings and possibly killing people. This was Laurie's first experience of war, he was impressed but somewhat bewildered, what made human beings want to kill each other. In the next four days which it took to reach Limehouse, unload the coal and start the return journey back north the pattern was the same. One could only describe it as a nightmare.

Many horrible events involving hundreds of very brave people, things that Laurie would never forget for the rest of his life, but they have no part in this story. London and the chaos that Laurie associated with it, lay many miles behind, their long winding way back to the Midlands had been quiet and fairly uneventful. There had been a few hold-ups but nothing serious. The *Orpheus* picked up some old rope with her propeller. Peter swam under the barge and cut it free. The barges, now travelling light stood high in the water, Making the task quite simple.

The barges being so high in fact, did cause a problem some days later. They had to pass under a low bridge on a section of the canal where the water was almost flood level. This sometimes happened in short stretches where too many vessels had passed going in the same direction. The continuous working of the locks created a false flood situation.

Arriving at the bridge late in the afternoon Father weighed up the possibility of getting under and decided to try the motor boat alone, It would be easier to navigate without the Butty in tow. After mooring the *Mars* alongside the bank, Father got underway again and slowly prodded the bows of the *Orpheus* at the narrow arch. He had the vessel plumb in the centre of the bridge but even so, she needed another three inches to get under. Father pulled the boat astern, came back alongside the *Mars* and made fast for the night. They would try again next morning. That evening Father and the three boys sat in the cabin having an early dinner.

The trip down to London had gone exceptionally well. Father was in a very congenial frame of mind, the boys were bantering each other as usual but also trying to think of something different to do. It was not often that they finished work so early in the day, It just so happened that Father had done some shopping here once, when they needed some stores and had found a very nice town with its own Cinema quite near to the canal. He suggested that all three might like to go, He would do the washing up but they would have to hurry or it might be too late.

Inside of five minutes they were on their way, bubbling over with excitement at the prospect of seeing a real live film. It was a very rare and special luxury. Even if the opportunity came they could seldom afford the money. Father's attitude towards worldly entertainment (as he described it) came last in the priorities of life. He was right of course, but the boys failed to see it that way. Arriving at the Cinema without difficulty, they were surprised to find the front doors closed. Lots of strange routines had to be adopted during the war. It was possible that lack of staff changed opening times or sometimes only one film would be shown, but starting later. This indeed was the truth of the matter, at the time only one man (a cleaner) was in the building and he was upstairs in the projection room. The boys decided to have a look round the back. On arriving at the rear exit doors, the boys found them wide open. They came to the conclusion that if they had to wait, it might as well be done in comfort. Inside the Cinema was dimly lit, it took a little while for their eyes to get used to the semi darkness, but once they could see enough to make out the aisle, it was a mad dash for the middle of the back row. Nicely settled in the comfortable armchairs they waited. It was just after six when the boys arrived and after half-past when the first people started to come in. The film was scheduled to commence at seven. A young lady had come in, walked down the side aisle and closed the exit doors, She failed to notice Henry, Peter and Laurie already nicely settled in the back row. The Cinema was short-staffed, this same lady sold the tickets. Apart from her there was only one projectionist and the cleaner. Henry was in favour of making their presence known but Peter and Laurie persuaded him that it might cause problems, after all they had come in the back entrance, so they laid back and enjoyed the film, Laurie's favourite 'a western' free of charge, guilty but innocent.

There had been a considerable drop in the water level by daybreak the following morning. Measurements that were cut into the bridge stonework showed a drop of eleven inches, compared with the previous day. It soon became apparent when all the shadows of darkness had passed away, there was now ample space between the bows of *Orpheus* and the bridge to motor safely through. Once clear, *Orpheus* and *Mars* were bound for Langley Mill to pick up another cargo of coal. Orders as to their next destination would await them there. Another journey was nearly completed.

Father was looking forward to a few days at home, some considerable time had elapsed since his last break. Laurie would be returning with him, the school holidays were coming to an end.

Before Laurie arrived back home to Sutton-In-Ashfield he was to have yet another new experience. For some reason or other the buses which linked up to make the journey possible were not running. This presented Father with a choice of waiting until they started again or walking and hitching lifts, whenever a car or lorry came along.

Laurie had tremendous admiration for his father who never appeared to have life made easy for him but nothing daunted him. They set out together, Father carrying a large case on his head and Laurie, doing his best to keep up with him, carried a small travelling bag which he kept changing from one hand to the other.

Strangers would stare in amazement at the sight. Father, striding along with a case balanced on his head. Laurie tried it many times without success. He trotted along behind putting up his thumb every time a vehicle came along. In the twenty mile hike, they used every form of transport one could think of: cattle truck, horse and cart, even a motorbike and side car, anything that saved walking and Father never complained once. If there was nothing available on wheels, they walked the twenty miles. This was Father's strength, he never gave up. Whatever the odds against him, his dogged faith kept him going. Laurie always remembered this, his respect for him never wavered, he held his father in the highest esteem for the rest of his life.

It was a Saturday and it took them from daylight till dark to reach home. Laurie was utterly exhausted but nevertheless very pleased to see his mother and sisters once more.

It seemed like a lifetime. Going to London and back on the canal barges had been a wonderful exciting time and it would never fade from his memory. The next day he slept late, as it was a Sunday and always a quiet day in the Gilson household.

When at home in the South of England they would all attend church but had not done so in the Midlands even so there was no spending allowed on Sunday, no games or football in the street. That left only sleeping or going for a walk and Laurie had walked enough the day before. There was no doubt in his mind where he was bound after lunch. Going to the Denby house in the past had been a regular and natural thing to do. Rita was his friend, going to call for her had become part of his routine day but now somehow it felt different. Was he really wanted? Had things changed while he had been away? Would Rita still want to see him? Her parents might consider him cheeky, a mere boy calling on a young lady to go out for walks, perhaps he should have sat on the village green and waited. As Laurie came closer his courage began to falter, the house was only a short distance away. He stopped and looked across at the Gypsy caravans, nothing much had changed there. He was on the point of turning round to go back when Rita called, she came out of the garden gate and down the road to meet him, putting her arms round his shoulders and squeezing him. She almost dragged him into the house. All his shyness vanished as Mrs. Denby made a fuss of him, he was treated like a hero.

CHAPTER EIGHTEEN

Laurie had so many exciting stories to tell and Rita was full of the holiday she had spent at Skegness. As usual, Mrs. Denby left them sitting on the carpet, munching cake and biscuits. Nothing had changed, they were completely happy in each other's company. Mrs. Denby sat and listened as they chatted away. She could understand the interest they found in each other. They were both natural story tellers, and the way in which they had met, cemented their friendship into a very special relationship. In that last week of the summer holiday, after returning from his adventures on the canal, Laurie enjoyed a short, lazy, relaxed time. He no longer endured that feeling of terror which had always preceded the start of a new term at school. He was far from being a brilliant scholar, but could now hold his own in most subjects. Certainly the main weakness in his educational achievements was hand writing, but this did not worry him unduly. Most of that week was spent in Rita's company. They were now very much aware of each other, and the fact that they were both growing up, but it never became a problem. The hours of contentment which they shared together for long periods of time were close, but innocent. There were moments of tenderness as they walked hand in hand through the fields which surrounded the town, but never any embarrassment. From that first evening (which neither had ever mentioned) they held hands quite naturally, it was as if the frightening tension of that strange introduction had formed a bond that wiped away the age gap and sealed their friendship.

Laurie went back to Hillocks School, after the summer holiday, a different person. Once again, there was a new teacher for him to get used to, but now this held no fears for him. When he walked into the classroom, there was just the normal curiosity, no longer the terrible fear that at one time would grip his stomach and leave his mind a blank. The teacher appeared in front of her pupils without any undue ceremony. Mrs. Phillips was a lady in the true sense of the word. She had a grown up family of her own and carried a quiet dignity about her which was instantly recognized and respected. Although Laurie was unaware of the fact at this time, the rest of his days in the Midlands were to be spent in this teacher's class, and very happy days they turned out to be. Mrs. Phillips insisted on student participation, her attitude to young people of this particular age group was that they should be involved with each other, in debates, charades, story telling, and testing their differing skills against each other.

Laurie thrived in this environment, his ability to stand in front of the class and tell story after story, without notes of any kind, completely captivated Mrs. Phillips. At first (before she had learned of his background) it occurred to her that the stories may have been taken from a book, the descriptions of certain scenes were so vivid that she could actually see the things happening. As time went by and she came to know Laurie well, it was obvious that he possessed a natural gift for story telling, and the varied experiences in his life gave him plenty to talk about. Mrs. Phillips came to the conclusion that Laurie Gilson was a most unusual character. His writing was atrocious, he held the pen incorrectly, and this she endeavoured to put right, but not very successfully, he would write a composition, with some skill, for a person of his age, but the problem was to be capable of deciphering the words. She was never able to give very high marks for his work, as it was so untidy. In spite of this, he progressed. Mrs. Phillips studied Laurie in all aspects of school work and play. She never ceased to be surprised at the vigour and enthusiasm with which he approached any type of sport or game, inside or outside the classroom his energy would appear to be endless.

Another unusual trait was his choice of friends, he appeared to be on good terms with the other children, but the boy he spent most of his time with was the unfortunate lad who suffered from epilepsy. His attacks now were few and far between, but when one did come, it could be quite violent. Mrs. Phillips had been forewarned what to expect by the headmaster, nevertheless she was astonished at the way Laurie just sat and held his friend's arm and shoulders, until the attack subsided, and then take him to the wash room to wash the froth from his mouth and face. She was impressed.

Laurie was to make two more voyages on the barges before leaving the Midlands.

Six very happy weeks passed quickly away. Laurie making the most of his opportunities to learn. He now made a point of reading every type of book that became available to him. His mother even went so far as to tell him that he was becoming a bookworm. This being not far from the truth, as Laurie would stay awake reading until the early hours of the morning,but he would never let this interfere with his sporting life. In three years he had evolved from a complete cabbage into a position where he had difficulty in making time for all his activities, indeed so much had happened in such a short time that Laurie began to wonder when, how, or where life was going to take him next. Unknown to Laurie his father had applied to the school headmaster for permission to take him out of class for the week coming up to half term. The barges were making a special trip to Birmingham, it was Father's intention to take the whole family with him. Permission was readily given. Laurie's story about his life on the barges had become quite popular. Mrs. Phillips suggested that it might be a good idea for him to write his adventures down, or even make notes for use later on. Laurie promised he would try, but winced inside at the thought of taking notes whilst working the cut.

The whole family set out on the bus for Langley Mill a

full week before the half term break. Laurie was pleased about this, it meant that he would be back by the time Rita returned from boarding school. The journey was uneventful, they arrived to find both barges fully loaded and ready to go. All five younger children of the Gilson family were now on the canal with their parents. Father shivered at the thought, it had not been his idea, he recalled the escapades of the three boys on the last trip down to London, what was it going to be like with two girls as well. He decided to hope, trust and pray, after all it was only for a week, surely not too much could happen in that time.

The weather was still holding fine as they let go off the mooring ropes. The little old Bolinder engine in *Orpheus* chugged away contentedly as she took the strain and pulled away from Langley Mill quay, it had been a good summer. Father prayed that it would hold. Standing at the helm of the motor boat with his father, Laurie could only marvel at the weight this tiny engine was pulling. Everything depended on this single cylinder diesel, it had to transport both barges, one hundred and twenty tons of coal, and seven of the Gilson family, to Birmingham and back. From the position where he stood, it was just possible to see the fly-wheel of the engine, so small, spinning so slowly. It did not seem feasible that so small an engine could accomplish so much. Mother had been preparing a long time for this special treat, it had been several years since she last had a holiday and it was her intention to make the most of it. The bed linen had always been carried on board both barges. Really it was just a matter of airing everything, the sheets and blankets never got grubby, Father saw to that. As soon as they were safely underway, she worked out the sleeping arrangements. The three boys, Laurie, Peter and Henry would sleep on the motor boat. Mary and Elizabeth were not too happy about the idea, but their bed would have to be where the boys normally slept, underneath Mother and Father, on the Butty boat. This was the girl's first experience of life as Bargees, the cramped accommodation was not to their liking.

Once the barges started to make progress through the lovely wooded countryside, the two girls forgot their moans and groans, even they had to admit that it was very beautiful. The whole family gradually settled into a set routine of working, eating and washing. It all had to be carried out in shifts, due to the confined living quarters, but it was accomplished quite successfully. It would take the barges some time to reach the junction where they changed course for Birmingham, the part of the canal now being navigated was in the area of the plum stealing escapade, in fact it was only another half mile to reach the bend where it actually happened, Henry had not failed to notice this. He was once again at the helm of the Butty boat, but this time he was alone. Laurie and Peter were painting on board *Orpheus*, Father was at the helm, and at the same time keeping an eye on them. The remainder of the family stood with him. Father was well pleased with the situation, things were working much more smoothly than he could possibly have hoped for. He pointed out things of interest to his wife and the two girls - for the moment he was content. One thing for sure, he was completely unprepared for what took place in the next few moments.

Henry decided that he would swing the Butty boat wide on the bend, it was his intention to explore the orchard for apples and pears, the juicy plums they had enjoyed on the last trip would be long gone as it was now late autumn. As the boats swung into the wide bend Henry put the helm hard over, the stern of the Butty almost disappearing under the trees. The difference in tension and angle on the tow was immediately obvious aboard the Motor boat. The whole family turned to witness a flying trapeze act, straight from the Big Top. Unfortunately for Henry, he had left one of the colourful water butts on top of the cabin, a branch swept the butt towards him, he let go of the helm and made a grab for it. With both arms outstretched, he failed to notice the next branch, which caught him under the armpits, lifting him clean out of the barge, leaving him suspended in mid air. Henry was not a swimmer, and as Laurie remarked at the time, neither was he a very good trapeze artist. Henry hung onto the branch in desperation, there was deep water six feet below him. Mother screamed for Father to save him, Peter muttered under his breath "Let him drown." One thing was for sure, he couldn't hang there much longer, he was tiring fast. Father was livid. Turning round would take much too long, he was unable to go astern without perhaps damaging the Butty.

Shouting orders for Peter to get out the long boathook, he rammed the bows of the motor boat into the canal bank. As soon as they hit the bank, Peter and Laurie jumped ashore, Father passed the boathook over to them, it was at least twenty feet long and should be long enough to reach Henry when he fell into the water. Henry hit the water just before they reached him, coughing and splashing, he came up for air, trying to dog paddle for the shore. The two boys came running back along the towpath, both wore short trousers, but they had to go into the water up to their chests, in order to reach Henry. Pushing the long wooden pole out at arm's length, they just made it and Henry was saved! Saved from the water perhaps, but not from Father's wrath. Poor Henry, wheezing from the canal water he had swallowed, was promptly treated to a sound thrashing for his trouble, it was definitely not one of his better days. Laurie could fully understand Father's anger at the loss of time, although he and Peter suffered hysterics that night as they went to bed. It had cost almost two hours of lost steaming in daylight hours, and time meant money. Even so, laying in their bunks that night, they laughed until their sides ached, at the thought of brother Henry, swinging in the branches of the trees like Tarzan - pity he didn't swim quite so well.

CHAPTER NINETEEN

Long before dawn, Father roused them, they had more than made up the time lost on the previous day, it was coming up to eight a.m., and the delicious smell of bacon wafting up from the cabin, told Laurie that mother was awake and preparing breakfast. Way ahead of them, an endless line of locks, winding up into the hill until they were lost in the morning mist. The mere presence of the locks promised a long day of hard physical effort and patience. This was the first of the two arduous tasks that had to be overcome before reaching their destination. To climb that hill, one lock at a time, took most of the day. Laurie may have lost count, or made a mistake, but he thought they numbered forty two. It proved to be a long tiring challenge, but it was overcome without mishap. By nightfall, the barges were through the locks, and heading for an experience that was new for all of them. There was always an element of danger on the canal. The locks themselves were quite harmless when handled properly and operated with care. Laurie remembered the fierce rushing water crashing over the weir on the River Trent. In times of flood these were very dangerous and frightening places.

When there was too much water, the canal became a hazardous raging torrent. If it ran too low, because of a dry summer, there were mud banks and underwater obstructions. The dangers, though not always obvious, nevertheless existed, and could cause disaster if not taken seriously. Laurie was aware of the famous Braunston tunnel that now lay just ahead of them. Stories had been told over and over again, of boats colliding in the tunnel. All the other narrow underground passages that had to be navigated were straight. This one was curved, which meant that any vessel entering, did so in complete darkness, and remained so until rounding the bend.

This difficult manoeuvre had to be completed before the other entrance became visible. Father decided that the barges would be breasted up to go through, this meant side by side, so he signalled Henry to come alongside with the Butty. Peter stood holding the bow rope ready to jump as soon as the two boats came together, but Peter, in spite of Father's shout of warning, jumped too soon, missed his footing and fell into the water with a loud splash. He was now between the barges and in danger of being crushed. Father, always alert to any danger, shot along the gang plank, and reaching over the side, grabbed Peter by the scruff of his neck, pulling him clear in the nick of time, before the two boats crunched together. Father, gasping for breath, and shaking at the thought of what might have happened, gave the bedraggled Peter a clip round the ear, for good measure. Both knew it had been a close call.

Laurie's heart was in his mouth as they entered that black void. It was as if the barges had been transported into another world, a world of dark, damp, filthy isolation. The silence shattered by the exhaust noise, which was magnified a hundred times in the enclosed space. Water that could not been seen, dripped like heavy rain from the roof and walls, soaking them to the skin. The sense of aloneness was both frightening and uncanny. Father had given strict instructions, nobody was to move about. Henry and Peter were stationed on either side, with rubber fenders, to prevent the barges getting damaged on the walls of the tunnel. It demanded a sense of feel, rather than sight, in these conditions. Laurie stood close to his father. He kept looking back at the ever decreasing spot of light, where they had entered this world of black darkness.

Then, suddenly, it had gone, they were rounding the bend of the tunnel. In books, Laurie had read about people living in caves, and going blind because they never came out into the light. Then it was just in books, now it was a reality. He thought how easy it would be to lose one's senses in this atmosphere, even to go mad. Then, suddenly, at the far end of the tunnel, a pinprick of light. They had completed the turn and were heading for light and sunshine. The worst part of the passage was over.

In fifteen minutes they were looking back up at the mass that was behind them. The sun was still warm on their backs and the journey nearly over. Soon the barges would be berthed at the chemical factory which was their destination. The whole cargo of coal which they carried had to be unloaded by shovel and wheelbarrow, and it had to be taken into the factory, some twenty yards from the canal bank.

At first, in the days when Laurie had been small and weak, he had been allowed to do his own thing, once they had reached their destination, but things had now changed, he was still quite small, but was growing more sturdy every day. Father thought it was time to test Laurie out and see just how strong he was. A barrow was half filled with coal, Laurie was given instructions on how to balance the one wheeled monstrosity along the plank, to the bank, and into the factory. At the first attempt, he was all over the place, but never lost any coal, shooting it out in the correct place, he returned for another load, and so the day went on. He was gifted with a natural balance, which made up for all his lack of size. Gradually, without him noticing the barrow was being topped up, Laurie was now carrying a full load of coal into the factory. Father smiled, the runt of the family had grown up quicker than expected. His mind wandered back to the days when his wife would rise from her bed every night to tend the needs of the sickly child who needed so much care. He watched Laurie run up the plank with a full barrow of coal, and marvelled at the change, he would never had thought it possible. Two days of hard work and the barges were clear, unloaded and washed down. Father was more than pleased, so far things had worked out very well. Laurie was now as good as an extra man. He found it difficult to understand how, in such a short time, a lad who was not expected to survive, had now become so energetic and vigorous, he slept that night a happy man.

CHAPTER TWENTY

The journey back to Langley Mill was enjoyable but uneventful, it was a relaxing time, there continued a holiday atmosphere, and a spirit of a mission completed. A time of family contentment, even Peter and Henry were at peace with each other, well, most of the time.

This time. Laurie and his sisters arrived back in Sutton-in-Ashfield without mishap, just in time for the half term holiday. For Laurie this consisted of only two days, but for Rita at boarding school it would mean a whole week at home. Hopefully Laurie would be spending some of that time at the Denby's, that is of course that Rita still wanted his friendship.

Because of all that happened over the past weeks, Laurie had not been able to pay a great deal of attention to his rabbits. The two large Flemish Giants had grown much too big for their hutch and changes had to be made before he was able to do anything else. Fortunately the wood yard that operated close by had plenty of spare planks ideal for extending the hutch. Laurie decided it would be quicker to make a new hutch, and as they had grown so large, let then live apart. This took most of the first day. Laurie had arrived home with his mother and sisters early on Sunday morning and he worked on the hutch until it was complete. It was much too late to think about going out and it had been a very long day. He had dinner with his family and went to bed tired, but content with the though that the Flemish Giants now had plenty of space and could live in comfort.

CHAPTER TWENTY ONE

Laurie wandered across to the village green. It was now Monday morning. He wanted to go straight to the Denby house, but something held him back. Sitting down on the grass he pondered, looking for the reason.

He realised that as he was growing older, he had become more aware of the fact that Rita was two years his senior. The question that worried him, and kept repeating over and over in his mind, was did she really want his friendship.

Apart from a few boys kicking a ball about on the green, the streets were pretty well deserted. Laurie considered asking the boys if he could join in the game. He loved football. A young woman had come down the hill from the direction of Low Street, which led to the centre of town. She was on the far side of the road but began to cross over when she reached the green.

Laurie had risen to his feet and was about to approach the boys, when the young woman waved. Glancing round, Laurie realized that he was the only other person on the green.

By this time, the young woman had come within speaking distance. Laurie was struck dumb, it was Rita!

She had on a grey skirt and white blouse, black stockings with heeled shoes, and her long blond hair was piled up on top - she looked almost six feet tall.

Laurie was lost for words as she put her arms round him, hugging him in that familiar fashion he had come to know so well.

Laurie hugged back, his blood raced, but he failed in his

attempt to speak, his throat had gone completely dry, so he just kept hugging, but his arms had tightened their grip. Rita looked down into his eyes laughing. "Somebody has been building muscles in the last two months" she said (ruffling his hair,) "and I thought you were going to neglect me."

Laurie relaxed his grip (not that he wanted to) and laughed with her. The relief that she still wanted his company brought his voice back.

"You look so different and grown up with your hair like that," he joked, "People will think I am taking my mother out for a walk."

They linked arms, and laughing together, headed for Rita's home, they never even discussed what was going to happen or what they were going to do. Their friendship was secure, and for the moment that was sufficient. Most of the leisure hours in the following week were spent together. Thinking about it later, Laurie was quite content that not many boys lived in the area. Who was he to complain?

CHAPTER TWENTY TWO

Laurie returned once more to school, he had not taken notes, as Mrs. Phillips, his teacher had suggested, but he was full of exciting stories to tell his classmates.

Frequently, when gaps between lessons would allow, Mrs. Phillips called on Laurie to stand in front of the class and tell of his adventures on the canal.

Occasionally she suspected there might be a certain amount of elaboration, but she found the stories so full of basic fact, that most of it just had to be true.

Laurie thoroughly enjoyed himself, it was such a contrast to those days when Mrs. Clark had been his teacher. Those horrible times when she would call him out in front of the class and ridicule him, make him try to read, when she knew how backward he was, and then the constant kneeling in the corner - it had brought sore knees and mental torture. They were bad days and he would never forget them.

The war situation had changed drastically. The threat of invasion had passed and news from battlefronts grew more encouraging every day.

Fishing on the south coast was gradually getting back to some sense of normality. Older fishermen who had remained in their home ports throughout the war, were managing to get a living without going far out to sea. Lack of fishing effort appeared to have increased the fish stocks tremendously and prospects looked promising.

Although nothing had been discussed with the children, Laurie overheard his parents say that it would be nice to go back home and all live together again. Whatever happened, Laurie realized that it would all take time and planning.

Father would have to get permission from the authorities to leave the canal, because it was listed as essential work. The coal was still in great demand all over the country. The canal was one of the cheapest and safest ways of transportation. It would obviously take some time to obtain his release.

While all this speculation was going on, Laurie got wind of another possible week on the canal. Strange as it may appear, Laurie received the news from his teacher, Mrs. Phillips.

After school had finished one afternoon, the teacher asked him to stay behind for a moment.

Laurie, on that particular day, had told one of his stories. He wondered what she could want, but was not unduly bothered, he seldom got into trouble these days, and certainly not with Mrs. Phillips.

When all the other children had left the classroom, she beckoned him over to her desk. "I understand from the headmaster that you are off on your travels again very shortly" she commented. Laurie must have looked a trifle blank, so she continued "Your father has asked if you may be excused school for a week. I have been informed that you will be taking coal to a brewery in Northampton. Make sure you stick to the lemonade, I like to keep a sober class. I shall expect plenty of stories when you get back, but no drunken brawling with your notorious brothers. Have a good time and come back safely". So Laurie was off once more.

CHAPTER TWENTY THREE

On the 16th of November, Laurie passed his eleventh birthday. It proved to be a very quiet day. If Rita had not been away at boarding school, she would almost certainly have come to tea, but her next holiday was four weeks away, Christmas only six, and the weather had become much colder.

Two weeks after his birthday, Laurie was once more travelling the now familiar route towards Langley Mill. As he looked out of the window, an occasional snowflake drifted past. The clouds looked very heavy and dark. Father predicted that there was bound to be snow before they reached their destination. He expressed the hope that it wouldn't be too much.

Father was right, it did snow, but fortunately only in the wind, which had freshened considerably. The wind continued to freshen until it reached gale force. It had developed into a horrible night by the time they boarded *Orpheus* and *Mars*.

Within ten minutes of their arrival, the cabin fire burnt merrily. One thing that never ran short was coal. On a night like this, they appreciated the fact.

Father had intended getting underway that night, he would have like to have covered a few miles just in case the snow set in thick, but with conditions as they were he decided against it, much to the relief of the boys who were nicely settled in warm blankets, wild horses would have been needed to drag them out of that cosy cabin.

Laurie had never experienced winter on the canal, nature consists of many different faces. Paradise that blooms in summer sunshine quickly fades when the harshness of winter comes. Yet still it retained a certain beauty, frost on trees and grass, ice on the stagnant water. When Father awakened them the following morning, it was daylight, a blanket of snow covered everything, the wind had died away in the night, leaving a clear, bright, frosty day. Laurie shivered, as he climbed up through the cabin hatch, his brothers were already on deck, preparing to get underway. To keep warm on a morning like this (as Laurie was to prove hundreds of time in his seagoing life) it was essential to keep moving in order to get the circulation going round the body.

Their work load increased considerably with the coming of the snow. They were already starting to move away from the quay. It was a case of all hands to the pump, figuratively speaking. Both barges needed clearing of all encumbrances, the little engine had more than enough to drive through the water, without having to contend with ice and snow.

The change to winter conditions altered the whole work routine and had a slowing down effect on every operation.

Peter's old bike remained stowed away down below. Even if the towpath had not been obliterated, it was impossible to ride on ahead to prepare the locks for the barges to enter.

Peter and Laurie attempted to speed up their progress on several occasions by running ahead, but it was terribly dangerous, to say the least, it only needed one false step to finish up in a ditch on one side, or the canal and ice cold water, on the other. Neither were very inviting, but of course, sometimes happened.

Fortunately the snow fall had not been too heavy. A clear sky and the sun providing a little warmth, as it rose higher, made the temperature rise and the snow begin to melt. Much against Father's wishes, later in the day, Peter made one attempt to use his bike, it ended in catastrophe. He had made just about a couple of barge lengths along the towpath, when he came a real cropper. It is possible that he might have got away with it, if, instead of turning round to wave, he had paid more attention to the difficult task he had undertaken. One moment he was waving merrily, the next he appeared to do a somersault in mid air, the wheels of the bike went up, poor Peter went down and down, and splash. He was unable to stop himself on the slippery bank. It was inevitable that his ultimate end would be the dark dirty waters of the canal.

Once again there were panic stations. Peter could swim, but the water was at freezing point, he may have injured himself when the bike turned upside down.

Father took immediate action. Putting the helm hard over, he pointed the bows of *Orpheus* at that part of the canal bank where Peter had disappeared. But he had no need to worry, Peter came up out of the water, just like the Sword Excalibur - hand raised to show that all was well. In minutes he was back aboard and in front of the fire, drying off.

Naturally he received the inevitable clip round the ear from you know who, but looking back, Laurie felt quite sure that this was Father's way of showing his relief that no serious harm had come to any member of his family.

Father seemed more determined than usual, despite the poor weather conditions, to push on with all speed. Although the old bike had to be stowed away for the time being.

Peter and Laurie were put ashore on the canal bank whenever convenient, to run on ahead of *Orpheus* and *Mars* in order to prepare the locks ahead.

Their journey continued without mishap. Each morning brought a heavy frost and bitterly cold temperatures. Ice patches formed on the water, not heavy enough to impede their progress, but made a nasty crunching sound as the bows of *Orpheus* forced a way through.

The sun came up bright every morning, and gradually as it rose in the sky, ice and snow would disappear. The air smelled clean and fresh - it was good to be alive.

Two days of determined progress and they were approaching their destination. Father had really forced the pace, travelling on into the night, they had made exceptionally good time, arriving at the Brewery in mid afternoon.

This was a one off trip to Northampton. The first sighting of the brewery as they turned into a small backwater, was impressive. It had its own quay, and was situated so close to the water, it gave one the impression that it was about to topple in. Even better still, a crane, with an automatic grab, stood waiting to unload the coal. Before the barges were moored alongside, hatches had been removed, ready to commence work. It was the best reception they had ever experienced, even the crane driver waited in his cab, anxious to make a start as soon as possible. Obviously they desperately needed the coal, and within minutes of berthing, the first grab, full of black shining nuggets, dropped into the massive hopper.

The fact that the coal was to be unloaded by crane, left Laurie to amuse himself most of the time, but he soon found himself a job.

Most of the people who worked in the Brewery turned out to be relaxed, easy going types. This could have had something to do with the serving of a pint of beer, four times a day to each man. Father remarked he was surprised they could even stand on their feet. The foreman laughed at Father's comments, but when told that neither he nor the boys drank beer, gallon jars of lemonade and ginger beer arrived as if by magic. It turned out to be an extremely well organised factory. One thing for sure, the barges had never been unloaded more quickly. Laurie got on famously with the men, he found himself a job straight away, in the brewery itself, for which he was paid half a crown for each of the two days they were there.

A great deal of the work was carried out on a gravity system, simple but extremely effective, when one considered the whole operation. The coal was fed into the hopper from a considerable height, it then slid down a series of chutes until it reached the furnaces.

At the other end of this enormous beer producing operation, Laurie found his job. Lorries came into the brewery through massive cast iron gates, stacked high with empty barrels, mostly ten or twenty gallon containers.

They would then back up to a canvas covered tunnel that led down into the factory. At the end of the tunnel, the barrels had to be turned round the opposite way and directed onto a long 'V' shaped gully, which ran all the way downhill, about one hundred yards. Here they were steamed, ready to be refilled. It was Laurie's job to twist the barrels at the top of the gully, facing them in the correct position - it was here he spent most of the two days.

It may not sound a very exciting job, but it was all go. The barrels kept coming all day, and men pulled Laurie's leg about his size. Every now and then he would kick a barrel into position. The men warned him that they could fight back if they got pushed around too much. Of course they were only joking. He sort of became a mascot, and they ribbed him all the time. But one of the barrels did bite back, well, in a way.

The men told him that he ought to wear gloves, but Laurie said he found it difficult to work with gloves on, and although they insisted it would be much safer, and made him wear them for a time, he soon had them off again. Gloves made his hands sweaty, he much preferred to have his fingers in the fresh air.

Laurie found out on the second day that the barrels really did have the ability to fight back. Well, not actually fight back, but at least do quite a lot of damage if not treated with respect.

A barrel was rolling towards him, he saw it coming and reaching out with both hands, placing them on the barrel, he attempted to twist it as usual. Laurie felt a prickly sensation in his fingers, he took his hands away quickly, they were dripping with blood, the container bristled with glass!

Laurie was rushed away to the first aid centre, although bleeding badly, the cuts in Laurie's hands and fingers were not too serious. He arrived, expecting to find just a room set aside for minor injuries, a first aid box and one of the workers, perhaps with a little first aid knowledge.

Much to his surprise, two qualified nurses occupied their own department and were on call twenty four hours a day.

Accidents happened frequently and the centre was well equipped.

Laurie, being the only patient that afternoon, received extra special care. Having washed away the blood and disinfected his hands. They decided that none of the cuts needed stitches, and as the bleeding had nearly stopped, it would be wise to leave them open for a time to allow them to have another look a little later when the cuts were completely dry.

Laurie sat back in an armchair, the nurses provided tea and biscuits and encouraged him to talk about his life on the canal.

Naturally once Laurie got started, there was no stopping him, he told them most of the funny stories and pranks that he and his brothers got up to.

He soon had them laughing about the old steam roller and the many times they had to be rescued from the canal after falling in.

The nurses thought that the story about brother Henry and his Tarzan act was hilarious and asked if they might meet his two notorious brothers later on. But first, one of the nurses (whose name turned out to be Susan) would take Laurie on a guided tour of the brewery, after which they would bandage his hands, provided no further treatment proved necessary.

An incident that had started in a very unpleasant way, resulted in Laurie having a most enjoyable and entertaining afternoon in Susan's company.

The brewery was enormous. Laurie had no idea that the factory was so big, or that it employed so many people. Susan led him through every department, explaining each different operation as they went along. The afternoon passed quickly by.

Much later, Susan took Laurie back to the casualty department, just to check that his hands were alright. The wounds were no more than deep scratches and would soon heal.

Laurie pointed out to the nurses that it was getting dusk, and if they wished to see the barges before dark, they would have to hurry. It would possibly be their only chance, as they would be leaving early in the morning. Unfortunately, the nurses explained that they were not allowed down onto the loading bay because of the coal dust, but that there was a window above the barges, where they could take turns to look out and wave. If Laurie went back straight away and told his brothers to look up, they would be able to talk to them from the window, Laurie hurried away. He arrived back aboard the barges to find that the coal had been unloaded. The boats were a hive of activity and just about ready to get underway.

Father was not too pleased that Laurie had been away so long without letting him know about his accident, but he was content with Laurie's assurance that it was nothing serious, his hands would heal in a couple of days.

It appeared that Father had known for some time that if they managed to unload quickly, another cargo was waiting only two hours steaming time away. Laurie understood now the reason for all the hurry. A return load meant double the money, but they were in a race with another pair of barges that were in the area, who also wanted the load.

Laurie hurried across to where Peter was preparing to cast off the mooring ropes. He helped to complete the task, and together they jumped on the Butty, and while the ropes were coiled and stowed, he told Peter what had happened. "Be sure and look up, just in case the nurses come to wave - pity we have got to leave so quickly".

The engine of the motor boat burst into life, they were on the move within seconds, Peter and Laurie at the helm of the Butty.

As the boats moved away from the quay, there came a shout from above their heads. Hanging out of the window and waving goodbye, were both Susan and the other nurse. The boys waved back. Laurie shouted his thanks, but any words were now lost in the noise of the motor boat's engine. They all kept waving until darkness closed in and blotted them from view.

CHAPTER TWENTY FOUR

This kind of experience was typical of life on the canal, arriving at different places, making new friends and dashing away without a chance to say goodbye properly.

Even now, as the barges steamed at top speed, it could well prove to be time wasted.

They headed for a destination that was unknown to the boys. Their intention to pick up a cargo which may have been taken at that very moment. They had no way of knowing where their rivals were, it was quite possible that the other two vessels had already arrived and started to load, but then again they could be just five minutes in front. If this proved the case, Father was going to be terribly disappointed.

Laurie thought about the situation they were now involved in. It has been referred to as a race. He smiled at the thought of anyone racing at a speed of approximately four miles an hour. It occurred to him that if one of them jumped ashore onto the towpath, they could possibly arrive at the pick-up point about twenty minutes ahead of the barges. He suggested this to Peter.

Peter's opinion was that even if it was legal in barge law, it would be against Father's principles. In any case he thought that they were bound for the granary and if he was correct, it was only three miles ahead.

Straining his eyes in the darkness, Laurie eventually picked out a cluster of lights on the port hand side, he told Peter, who confirmed that if his supposition was a right one. This was the place. He asked Laurie if there appeared to be any low lights other than the cluster. Laurie's reply was in the negative.

Peter's guess had been correct. Close to an hour later, they berthed at a small but modern quay, it had the appearance of recent completion, and could have been made to measure for the two barges to lay alongside. Father went ashore just as soon as the vessels were safely moored. He came back in minutes with a smile on his face, it was now five thirty in the evening and just a few weeks to Christmas, they had won the race, and would commence loading at six the following morning, they could now relax and have a meal. He instructed Henry to stop the engine.

In the silence of the night that followed, they could hear in the distance the sound of another engine. Their arrival had been none too soon, one hour later and the load would have been lost.

As they sat in the tiny cabin that evening, enjoying a feast fit for a king, Father decided to break the news.

He was obviously in good humour, they had secured a return load, which, if delivered safely, would provide enough finance for all the plans he had made for the future.

He decided that this was as good a time as any to tell the boys.

Father seldom discussed the family situation with the boys, but as this was going to affect the whole of their future lives. He had been waiting for the right moment to tell them. This would be the last voyage they would make on the barges, he had received his release from the Government, as soon as the last cargo had been delivered, the barges would return to Langley Mill, and eventually the whole family would be returning to their home town on the south coast.

The boys just sat looking at each other in silence, they were lost for words, each with his own thoughts as to the changes it would make in their own personal lives. For Laurie it meant another new school, it was the end of his adventures on the canal. It would mean that he would possibly never see Rita again, and his heart sank. He had always longed for the day when they would be able to return home to the sea, the plans he had dreamed about, the adventures that he had been able to see for the future, but now he was faced with reality, it was all going to happen soon, not years ahead, but soon.

Peter and Henry were also quiet, they enjoyed their own personal lives and friends. Father had dropped a bombshell in their lap, there were so many questions to be asked, so many queries as to what the future held for each one of them, but for the moment they were silent, the questions would have to wait, the first priority was sleep. They had all worked hard since early morning, loading at six the next day condemned them to another extra long day. It would be easier to think and take in the full significance of Father's news when they had a full night's sleep behind them.

The next morning at six a.m. sharp, the loading started. The barges had never carried grain before, it was loose in bulk, which was most unusual. Father was not too happy about this, he had expected the load to be in sacks, but as the town was only two days away from the loading point, he accepted that the risk was minimal, not much could happen in two days.

The loading time was the quickest they had ever encountered, both barges were loaded and ready to get underway in under four hours. The grain came out of the hopper so fast and moved so easily, that it took great care not to spill or overfill each section.

At ten o'clock, the barges were full and ready to go, Father had no intention of wasting time, and very soon they were underway. They pushed on with all haste, travelling south towards London. Come nightfall, half of the distance had been covered, the weather had been extremely kind to them, it was bright and sunny with quite a heavy frost at night. Temperatures were low, but not low enough to freeze the canal, any ice that formed in the night quickly melted during the day.

Late afternoon on the day after loading the grain, they approached their destination. The last voyage of their days on the canal were nearly over, there was a sad feeling in the air.

Unloading the grain shipment turned out to be a mere formality, carried out by a suction pump system. It was a strange coincidence that the last voyage on the barges was definitely easier than anything they had experienced before. Laurie and his brothers sat on top of the Butty boat's cabin, like spectators at a football match. In a few hours the whole operation had been completed, and once again they prepared to get underway.

It had all become routine procedure in their lives, carried out automatically and without fuss. In minutes, the *Orpheus* had *Mars* in tow, once more they were chugging north toward Langley Mill, but this time there was a marked difference, it would be the last time.

That last journey proved to be very nostalgic. Each familiar object, lock or town, or area where some funny or strange incident had occurred, it was remembered and noted. They all realised the possibility that not one of them would ever pass that way again.

The passage was a smooth, relaxed one, without mishap. Crossing the River Trent for the last time brought back many memories, but no undue problems. It struck Laurie that everything was being made easy so that the memories they carried away with them, would be pleasant and continue to be so.

Laurie stood in the stern of the Butty as they approached the last bridge under which they would pass. Standing on the centre of the bridge, waving to the boys, was a middle-aged lady, she appeared to be singing. *Orpheus* had gone through the bridge and was already on the other side. For just about a minute, with one barge on either side, Peter and Laurie lost the exhaust noise, all was peace and quiet, apart from the lady chanting. The boys grinned at each other and waved when they heard the words that she chanted. "*Orpheus* and *Mars*, *Orpheus* and *Mars*, Milky Way, Milky Way, *Orpheus* and *Mars*:"

Laurie had never thought of the barges in that light before, it sort of gave their names a majestic quality, made them sound grand, not just a couple of old boats that worked the Grand Union Canal.

Laurie could not help feeling that the lady singing those special words, so close to the end of this phase in his life, was meant to be - so applicable, so fitting, and yet so sad, as they came in sight of Langley Mill. In no time the long narrow boats would berth alongside and the engine stopped for the last time. It was all over.

CHAPTER TWENTY FIVE

As Father wanted to put the barges in apple-pie order before they actually left for home, he decided that they would stay overnight, with the intention of catching the first bus on the following morning.

Laurie was pleased about this, as there were not many jobs that he could get involved in. It gave him a chance to wander round all the old haunts and browse over the moments of interest, and indeed much happiness came flooding into his mind. He looked at the rows of coal trucks, the big hopper that loomed over the barges at this very moment, as if threatening to load them, whether they wanted or not. The long metal chutes that swung from side to side, guiding the coal into the barges, filling up all the available space. Standing in the quiet of the evening, observing these things formed a mental picture he would carry with him for ever.

Circumstances had brought him to a way of life which he would never have thought possible, a way of life which was all good grounding for his future, (although of course he could not know this at the time). At this moment it was beyond his comprehension that life was going to change completely.

In his young heart Laurie had almost become a Bargee. Never to see the cut nor the barges, locks, tunnels, or the beautiful scenery again, was unthinkable.

It only came home to him now as Father put the padlocks on the hatches. It was eight a.m. the following morning, in twenty minutes the bus should arrive to take them away. All four of them stood looking down at the narrow boats which had been their homes. Cases in hand they turned away, as if in a dream. Only now did the truth really come home to them. Not one of them spoke. Laurie had a lump in his throat, he knew that Father, Henry and Peter felt the same. They turned away from the quay towards the waiting bus. Laurie found it difficult to make up his mind, were they going home, or leaving home perhaps he would never know the answer.

CHAPTER TWENTY SIX

The bus wound its way through the narrow country lanes, the driver was obviously taking care, there had been a heavy frost and the roads were icy.

Their travels had taken longer than expected because of the extra shipment of grain.

Two weeks and it would be Christmas, Laurie had hoped for a white one, but the snow which had fallen on the outward bound bus ride had cleared, leaving the weather bright but very cold.

The fact that they were almost a week later than expected, getting back, had taken Laurie up to the Christmas holidays, there would be no more school for him now until after the break.

Although wheels had been set in motion for the Gilson family to return south, there was a lot of planning and preparing which had to be carried out, before this could happen.

Laurie arrived back at their present home in Sutton In Ashfield with his father and brothers later than expected. They should have reached the house in Grover Street by mid afternoon, but due to problems with the buses once again, they didn't arrive until late on the Saturday night. This was nothing unusual, just something they had learned to live with, it was a case of fitting into the system that war had forced on everyone.

Father insisted that it was much too late for discussion over supper. It was to be 'early to bed, early to rise, makes a man healthy, wealthy, and wise,' one of his many favourite sayings, but one which throughout his life Laurie had many reasons to doubt, but for the time being Father's word was law, and he wouldn't be the one to argue against that law.

The following morning Laurie did awake bright and early, but it had nothing to do with the family. He new that Rita would be home from boarding school for the Christmas holiday and if there were any chores to be done, he wanted them quickly out of the way.

It had been several weeks since they had last been together, Laurie was always concerned that the longer they were parted, the more difficult it was for him to pick up where they had left off in their relationship, but as he kept reminding himself, Rita did not appear to have this problem.

Most of the morning had gone by the time Laurie had finished helping his mother. There was also a family conference. Father explained that he would be returning to the south coast accompanied by Henry and Peter to prepare the house (which had been empty for a long time) and also to sound out the possibilities regarding the fishing. The rest of the family would follow later, if all went well.

Laurie was content for the time being, to all intents and purposes it would run into many weeks before he once again had to change home and school, it had always been uppermost in his mind that some day he would return to the sea, and this was even now his greatest wish and outweighed all else.

So much had changed, circumstances had changed, relationships had changed, more drastic than anything else, Laurie had changed. He thrived on physical challenge and loved rough games. To climb trees, ropes or buildings, was meat and drink to him. He never appeared to run short of energy or tire of any game. But Laurie had also become an addict to books, he loved to read adventures of any kind, but his special favourites were about the sea. His reading had improved beyond recognition in no more than a year. This was mainly due to his close relationship with Rita.

Laurie decided to wait until after lunch before venturing

round to the Denby house in search of Rita. There were so many jobs that built up while he was away and they all had to be attended to. Laurie now owned Flemish Giant rabbits, he constantly got his leg pulled because he boasted about their size, but they really were beautiful animals, he was very proud of them and took great care cleaning out their hutches. This was the reason he had such a full morning. The job was eventually completed to his satisfaction, lunch out of the way and he was free for the afternoon.

As Laurie approached Rita's house, he again experienced that strange feeling of doubt, in spite of the fact that he was always made so welcome. Did her parents think him cheeky to come calling, the way he always had done. Once again he hesitated, With his hand on the garden gate, reluctant to enter.

Even if there was any intention on his part to make a quiet escape, and hope for a casual meeting, the matter was taken out of his hands.

Strong hands gripped him by the shoulders, "Caught, breaking and entering," said Mr. Denby as he propelled Laurie towards the front door. "Our wandering hero returns once again from his adventures on the high seas," he said, laughing and squeezing Laurie at the same time.

If Laurie had any doubts about his welcome, he needn't have bothered. Rita was already halfway down the front path to meet them, and he was quickly smothered in the welcome of the whole family.

Laurie, as always was overcome by the fuss they made of him. He was drawn into their family circle so easily, it was as if they considered him to be adopted, and had a permanent home whenever he chose to come and visit.

Hot drinks, cakes and biscuits were soon on the table. It was as if Laurie had never been away, and the stories flowed easily in the homely atmosphere.

Laurie looked at Rita while the conversation flowed and realised how much she had matured. Her speech and her manner were that of an educated young lady who had advanced well into her studies. She had obviously made the most of the opportunities open to her. There was no doubt in Laurie's mind whatsoever, that Rita was going to be a very intelligent and sophisticated lady.

Laurie had decided that for the moment he would not mention the question of his moving back south, after all nothing at this stage of the proceedings affected him and might not materialise. The last thing he wanted to do was upset his present active enjoyable way of life, without good cause. But he had not allowed for the fact that his mother and Mrs. Denby had become good friends, he had no way of knowing that Rita and her mother and father had already been told.

While they chatted about the barges, canal, and Christmas being so close, Laurie intercepted several doubtful glances, especially between Rita and her mother. It appeared that they were uneasy about something. He was not kept in suspense for long.

As usual, the two youngsters were left on their own to amuse themselves. This was a time when they would discuss books and things of mutual interest, a time when Laurie learned more than he could at school. Having Rita as a friend was the equivalent of having private tuition, but on this occasion Rita made no attempt to speak, she was waiting for Laurie .

They were laying on the carpet in front of a blazing fire, looking into each other's faces. Laurie was surprised to see that her lovely grey green eyes were moist with tears, it was the only time since their first strange meeting that this had happened - he was taken off guard.

They had not been alone together for many weeks, but such was their relationship that Laurie quite naturally put his arms round her shoulders, resting her head so that their faces were touching. He stroked her long blond hair, then kissed her cheek. Laurie wanted to comfort her, but was searching for words, then at last Rita came to his rescue.

"I know that you are going away and we shall never see

each other again," she said, her voice was quiet but controlled. "Why didn't you tell me?" Then Laurie understood. Rita and her parents had known all the time, his mother must have told them.

Laurie explained that nothing was definite at the moment, and that it might not happen at all. He valued their friendship too much, spoiling Christmas for something that might never come about, had made him stay silent.

Laurie was still very young, but he was also very disturbed at the effect Rita's warm body, pressed against his, was having. The turmoil inside him was unbearable. How could someone as lovely as Rita have such strong feelings and care about a boy as young as he.

Gently Laurie held Rita away, feeling guilty. He was ashamed at the thoughts in his mind, but Rita understood, she leaned forward and kissed him on the lips, making Laurie's heart pound. The only other woman ever to kiss Laurie was his mother, but not like this.

Rita started to speak and the magic moment had passed, she was trying to explain her feelings without sounding silly.

"Every hour that we have spent in each other's company since that first horrible night we met, has brought me happiness. I have never tried to make other friends or seek for companions of my own age, (apart from school). We have enjoyed a special relationship which has given me all the things which have made me content. I know that eventually you will be going back to your home town, life will change completely for both of us, there is nothing either of us can do about these things, but I shall miss you terribly." Laurie still held Rita's hands in his own, but he had no chance to answer, there was a movement at the door and Rita's parents entered the room and sat down, the youngsters hands were still clasped together.

Rita's parents were two of the nicest people Laurie had ever met. Even at a moment of time when there was perhaps much they could have said, the only comment Mr. Denby made was "Don't worry, we understand, if you do return to your home town Laurie, we shall miss you almost as much as our daughter will."

They all enjoyed many happy moments in each other's homes after that day. It turned out to be almost spring before Laurie's family prepared to move, and those months in between were very happy. Different from those first days that Laurie had spent in the Midlands. It was strange how fate takes a hand in the events of some peoples lives.

CHAPTER TWENTY SEVEN

The Gilson family had become quite well known, and made many friends in the three years that they lived in the Midlands. Many they would keep contact with for the rest of their lives.

Laurie stayed at Hillcocks School with Mrs. Phillips as his teacher for the remainder of the time spent at Sutton In Ashfield staying in contention with the rest of his classmates in most subjects, making the most of every sporting opportunity that came his way, life was good and he was happy.

Laurie and Rita were able to continue their close friendship at half-term and again for the first part of the spring holiday. They never again discussed Laurie's going away, but made the most of any time that was left to them - they were always very close.

Time has no meaning when life is full of purpose. Laurie began to realise this as the days, weeks and months slipped quickly away.

He would never be a brilliant scholar, but had gradually developed a joy for living. What he lacked in brain power, he made up for in the energy he generated into all the things he attempted to do. His efforts at school were recognized by Mrs. Phillips, his teacher, who knew and understood his background. The work that he put into each day's studies brought Laurie tremendous satisfaction and an inner contentment, which he never would have thought possible.

By this time his reading and arithmetic had improved so much that he could compete with most of the boys in his age group, and this had all been achieved in three years, he had good reason to be satisfied with the progress made. He was now eleven years and five months.

The spring had arrived before Laurie was ready for it, there lurked in the back of his mind that terrible misery he had endured as a little boy in his home town. Was it possible that after all the work put in and happiness now enjoyed, that he might be returning to similar circumstances. It gave Laurie much food for thought, and an empty feeling in his stomach.

The date had now been fixed for their departure, most of the family belongings had been packed ready to go. It was now Thursday in the second week of May. They were due to leave on the following Monday.

Laurie had informed Rita's parents. They had assured him that Rita would be home from school for the weekend. It was not usual at this part of term, but she had received special leave for the occasion and would arrive home on the Friday evening. At least he would have the chance to say goodbye.

Laurie bade farewell to his teacher, Mrs. Phillips, on the Friday afternoon. She expressed her sadness at his leaving, adding that she was going to miss his stories about the canal, but that they would always stay in her memory. She promised that she would always remember him as one of her most interesting pupils. After wishing him well for the future, they shook hands and parted, never to meet again.

CHAPTER TWENTY EIGHT

Rita arrived home at tea time on Friday evening. She came looking for Laurie immediately. The weather had been dull and miserable. In fact, when Rita knocked on the door, it had just started to rain. After greetings had been exchanged with the family, they decided to return to Rita's home straight away, as the dark clouds appeared to be increasing, and as Laurie put it afterwards 'it was far more peaceful at the Denby house.'

Mrs. Denby received Laurie in the normal overwhelming way he had come to expect from her, and quickly they were into planning the weekend. None of them wanted to discuss the fact that it was possibly the last of its kind they would ever spend together. Most important for the time being, were two whole days in which they could enjoy each other's company.

Tomorrow being Saturday, if the rain stopped, they would go for a picnic. Sunday, the last day, Laurie would spend with the Denby family, as he had so many times before. They talked on about school and friends. Only when future holidays were mentioned, did the room go quiet. Mrs. Denby decided to make some more tea.

As it rained hard on the following morning, the plans were reversed, Laurie stayed at the Denby house all day, thoroughly enjoying himself in their company. Their home had become like his own. The four of them would play cards for hours, and such pleasant moments were only interrupted to take tea, eat cake and biscuits, or dig into an enormous home-made pie. Mrs. Denby was an excellent cook and loved to see Laurie's considerable appetite satisfied.

It was late evening when Laurie made his way home, the rain had ceased in the mid-afternoon and as daylight faded and shadows began to haunt dark corners, the moon came up full and clear, it promised a bright sunny day for his last in the Midlands, he hoped so, for the sake of the picnic. He had left Rita and her mother preparing for the next day's feast.

Sunday proved to be as fine as Laurie had hoped. He was awake early, anxious not to be late. He had arranged to call for Rita at nine sharp, if the sun was shining, and it certainly was. Already he could feel the heat on his back as he walked up the street, dressed in only shirt, shorts and plimsolls. He new it was going to be a gorgeous day.

Rita stood at her garden gate, ready. If the size of the basket was anything to go on, there would be no shortage of food. Laurie was expecting Rita's parents to come, but Mrs. Denby saw them off at the gate, saying they had relatives to visit, and to have a good day.

It took nearly thirty minutes to reach the spot they had chosen, there were green fields close to a lake, not frequented by many people and sheltered by a small wood on the town side. They had walked round the lake many times and noted this place as being ideal to have a picnic. It was certainly a lovely setting.

The large blanket Rita had brought with her was spread on the grass. A table cloth was arranged at one side of the blanket and the banquet prepared. They lay back in the warm sunshine, lapping up the stillness and smell of the rich fragrant country air.

Laurie and Rita combined all the enjoyable moments of the months they had known each other into that one last day.

After the sun had warmed their skin to the point where it began to tingle. They walked through the woods in the shade of the trees, then raced across lush green grass to stand in the water of a mist covered lake, wading into the cool still water, until their cloths prevented them going further and deeper.

It was well past lunch time when they eventually tucked into the food. The day was passing much too quickly for both of them. Mrs. Denby had worked wonders, they slowly savoured the contents of her hamper until only crumbs remained. Rita turned the empty basket upside down, laughing as she did so. "My mother would love to cook for you every day."

She stopped laughing, realizing it was the last time. Suddenly there was silence and neither of them could find words to express their feelings.

Laurie jumped to his feet, pulling Rita with him. "Come on, I'll race you to the wood and back" he shouted, as he started to run.

Taking her by surprise, Laurie had gained a three yard start, but he needed all of that. They had nearly two hundred yards to cover and Rita was very fast. He should have chosen a longer distance because of his staying power - already he could hear her feet pounding the ground just behind him.

When he turned at the first tree, Rita was only a yard behind, it was going to be a close thing. Laurie had almost reached the blanket, when Rita grabbed him from behind, they fell in a heap, with Rita on top, gasping for breath.

They had no control over what happened after that moment. Still only children and innocent, they were also two very energetic and vigorous young people.

Laurie waited, but Rita made no attempt to move away. His heart was pounding and his body was rigid. Neither had much on in the way of clothes, and as they lay locked together, Laurie felt the trembling of Rita's body as the rest of their garments were kicked aside.

Laurie's strict upbringing stopped him making the first move, but now he was lost. The only thing that mattered in the world at that moment was this lovely girl, naked in his arms. He gently rolled over, they were both incapable of speech as he pressed into the softness of her body. With their lips touching and a stifled whisper of a gasp from Rita, they were transported into an unknown world of magical mystery.

Neither of them knew or cared how long they lay in each

other's arms, or how many times each was consumed with pure ecstasy, the sheer joy of their first love was unbelievable. It was much later than expected when eventually they arrived back at the Denby house. Mrs. Denby made no comment as she opened the door. It might have been the feeling of guilt that came over him when she looked in his eyes, but he was sure she knew what had happened, but nothing was said as they drank the ritual cup of tea, and it was Rita who was bubbling over with conversation about the events of the day. It was at times like this that her maturity showed and Laurie could only gaze in wonder at her composure. Laurie stayed at the Denby house late that night. He had no intention of leaving until the very last moment. His mother had not given specific instructions for him to be home at any particular time, and as this would be the last time, he was going to make the most of it.

Mr. Denby had arrived back soon after Laurie and Rita, there was much talk about the future and what was likely to happen after Laurie and his family had left the Midlands. The fact that this was only hours away would not penetrate Laurie's mind. Just the thought of leaving after all that had happened at the picnic, made everything appear like a dream. Laurie tried to pull himself together, he was well aware that although the conversation continued to flow in the little front room, his contribution was almost nonexistent, somehow, as yet, for him there was no tomorrow.

Mr. & Mrs. Denby left the children alone to say their farewells. Rita walked Laurie to the gate. What could they say to each other? Everything had been said and done much earlier.

Promises were made as the two youngsters stood in the dark, holding each other close.

There were serious pledges that both intended to keep, if fate would allow, but it was to be some years before either would meet again, although of course, they could not know this at the time. Eventually Laurie took his leave and walked slowly home.

There was little sleep that night for Laurie. He twisted and turned all through the long hours until daylight began to break. Inside him there was a deep feeling of guilt that was to stay with him for many months after, but in spite of this, he would not have changed one moment of that wonderful day. It was a day in his life that even Laurie with his vivid imagination, could never make up.

CHAPTER TWENTY NINE

The Gilson family arrived back at the old house in the south of England to a great welcome. Father, Henry and Peter had been settled in some time, Father had started fishing, in partnership with an old friend. While the two boys had taken temporary jobs gathering cockles for a distant relation and were doing quite well.

For Laurie there were so many changes, he was finding it very difficult to fit into the new scene. Considering the mixed emotions experienced on the day before leaving the Midlands, his life at this moment had once more become a turmoil. For him, that picnic and all that had taken place, could not have come at a worse time. After all, he was still only a young lad, and in spite of the many experiences throughout his short life, that last day had been a major upheaval.

The war was about to reach its peak, air raids were continuous, and even in those first few days at home, much of the night was spent in the air raid shelter which had been built in the back yard. The planes were constantly backwards and forwards, whilst during daylight hours dog fights became a common occurrence. The boys would stand watching, as the enemy planes came up the River Thames and were intercepted before they could reach London.

Laurie first attended his future school on the Monday, one week after their return. He was taken in and introduced to the Headmaster, a Mr. Haxall, who it turned out already knew most of the family history. He had taught three of Lauries brothers in the past and expressed his sentiments that 'as good as them and better would do'. As the youngest male of the clan, he expected the last to be the best, and looked forward to a happy relationship together.

All the boys gathered for assembly, which lasted some twenty minutes, and then marched off to their individual classrooms.

Laurie had been shown which group of boys to stand with and told that after assembly he was to return and wait outside the headmaster's study, from there he would be taken and introduced to his new teacher.

It was some considerable time before a prefect arrived to carry out the duty, and Laurie was getting nervous, he thought they might have forgotten him and some of his old trepidation about school began to return, but the prefect was relaxed and friendly, chatting away as they climbed one flight of stairs, walked past several rooms in a long corridor, eventually stopping outside 'One C'.

The prefect knocked at the door, a lady's voice said "Enter." You could have pushed Laurie over with a feather, when he realized that the teacher sitting at her desk, was none other than Mrs. Clark, his old enemy of many years. The surprise must have shown on his face. He stood with his mouth open and a shattered look on his face. This was the last thing he had expected:

Mrs. Clark had obviously known that Laurie Gilson was coming into her class that morning and was well prepared. She directed him to sit at an empty desk at the front of the room, right under her nose. She looked down at him now with those cold eyes that he remembered so well, then, as Laurie fully expected, in that steely voice he had feared so much in those bad old days, she said "Get out your reading books, Gilson, we have now reached page four, but just as a change for the rest of the class, you will come to the front and read from chapter one, it should only take a few minutes and will bring you level with the rest of our class."

The smile on Mrs. Clark's face spoke for itself. Laurie had

seen it so many times. He was determined to wipe that smile away once and for all. Picking up the book, he walked to the front of the room and slowly opened the first page.

Curiously as it may seem, at that critical moment, standing in front of the class with Mrs. Clark at his mercy, Laurie's mind wandered very briefly over those years of hard work, the patient teaching of Mr. Jones, of the kindness and understanding from Mrs. Phillips. Then Rita, who was so intelligent, and through their friendship had helped him emerge from a wilderness of loneliness to a world of light and understanding. He was dreaming again, the sharp voice of Mrs. Clark interrupted the dream. "We are waiting Gilson," she said. "I take it you are still as lazy as ever in spite of all I tried to teach you.

Laurie came out of his dream with a jolt, then in a clear steady voice began to read. He neither hurried or hesitated. He made sure his punctuation was perfect. Never in all his school life had he taken so much care to be absolutely correct.

It was now Mrs. Clark who listened, with her mouth wide open. At first she couldn't believe her ears, but as Laurie carried on reading, she sat back in wonder and allowed him to continue. It had been her intention to let him stumble through a couple of lines, but the progress this boy had made was in itself a lesson for the whole class. She listened with pleasure until he reached page four - at this point Laurie stopped, as instructed.

To the other boys in the room, who had no idea of the feud that had gone on for so many years between Laurie and Mrs. Clark, the incident had little significance, but from that moment on, the light shone out of Laurie's eyes, as far as Mrs. Clark was concerned.

Their relationship was one of complete harmony, although she did complain many times about his work being untidy.

Southchurch Hall School was to be Laurie's place of learning for the next two and a half years.

It was here that he would complete his very short educational life, and once he had settled in, he made use of every second, getting involved in anything that presented a challenge. His constitution thrived on work and sport.

He took part in debates and discussions, loving each minute, sometimes staying after school time in order to finish a project. There was so much to learn in such a short time.

His achievements in the gymnasium were soon recognized, and in time he was offered evening classes for a seven year course, which he accepted with enthusiasm. Naturally at that point in time, every activity lacked the sophistication which is now taken for granted. The gym was only equipped with the very basics - boxhorse, springboard, and mats for ground work. But for Laurie these were enough to give him hours of pleasure, and eventually to bring his body into a reasonable state of physical fitness. As a result of this, his ability on the field of sport also improved, and he rapidly climbed the ladder to success and happiness, as the days, weeks and months sped away.

Laurie changed his class as progress determined, but it made very little difference as he was well known to all the teachers in the school. That terrible feeling which always came with the arrival of a new teacher, or a change of any sort in the system, ceased to exist.

Life had now become good for Laurie, he was in the second highest class in the school, under the supervision of a Mr. Griffith, a very keen footballer, but also the English and handwriting master for the whole school.

He constantly complained about the quality of Laurie's handwriting and his untidiness, but they were good friends, mainly because of their mutual love of football. He took great pleasure in attending sports lessons whenever possible, and would stand on the line shouting advice, getting as much enjoyment out of the game as the boys themselves. He was a good teacher and popular with most of the boys.

As Laurie approached the time when he would go into the top class and his last year at school, he experienced the greatest pleasure since his arrival at Southchurch Hall, and brought about the crowning moment of his whole school life. Every Monday morning, the whole school gathered in assembly for prayers and special announcements. The morning in question was no different from any other, apart from the fact that Mr. Haxall, the headmaster, advised all present that a new head teacher had been appointed to the school and would take over the top class immediately.

Laurie was all attention - this was going to affect him. Mr. Haxall carried on speaking. The teacher was a man of much experience and the school were fortunate in obtaining his services, he should have arrived in time for assembly, but must have been delayed. Mr. Haxall was possibly the only person in the hall who had noticed a tall silver grey haired, athletic looking man slip in at the back. He addressed him straight away.

"Come forward Mr. Jones and let me introduce you to the boys." As he turned, Laurie hardly dared to hope, it couldn't be his Mr. Jones, not here at Southchurch. But sure enough, striding swiftly down the centre of the hall, with that purposeful action Laurie knew so well, was the man for whom he had so much respect, no, it was more than respect, he almost idolized this man, but had never expected to see him again.

Mr. Jones was introduced and said a few brief words to the effect that it was a pleasure to be back at the school where he had taught many years ago, and to serve under Mr. Haxall, who was an old friend, and as he spoke, his eyes went along the rows of boys standing in the hall, looking for familiar faces.

Laurie wondered if Mr. Jones would recognize him. It had been over three years and Laurie had grown considerably in that time. Mr. Jones had just come to the point of saying that he would be pleased to meet old friends and looked forward to making new ones, when his eyes rested on Laurie. Just for a second he hesitated, then carried on with a few more well chosen words. He sat down next to Mr. Haxall and out of sight from Laurie, who by this time was full of excitement at the thought of a year, his last year at school, which was to commence quite soon, and it was to be in the care of his favourite teacher. He made up his mind that he would try to speak with Mr. Jones at lunch time, if he got the opportunity, after all it would only be a short time now to the end of term, and he was going to be his teacher.

Laurie stayed in the empty classroom at playtime, he had much to think about and wanted to consider what this fresh turn of events would mean to him. The return of Mr. Jones to be his teacher for his last year in school, was beyond anything he could have hoped for.

The door opened and closed without Laurie noticing. "Are you too busy to greet an old friend, Laurie, or had you forgotten me?" said Mr. Jones with a smile on his lean face.

Taken off guard, Laurie hesitated for just a fraction of a second, then grasping both hands that were stretched out towards him, they clasped each other in a long warm embrace. The pleasure on the faces of both teacher and pupil was obvious. Laurie, as usual at a time such as this, was lost for words, but his grip on the teacher's hands told everything.

Mr. Jones asked about Laurie's family and how long they had been back from the Midlands. Laurie responded with the latest news on his family's movements, telling the teacher how often he had thought about him, and still continued to practice with the circle of numbers. He quite truthfully told Mr. Jones that his school life had been a misery up until the moment they had met, and now after all this time, to know that his last year at Southchurch was to be spent with Mr. Jones as his teacher, was like a dream, it was unbelievable.

The arrival of Mr. Jones completed the preparation for a very happy last year at school as far as Laurie was concerned. They met and talked whenever possible, although as yet he was not in the top class. This did not prevent Laurie from slipping into Mr. Jones' room at odd times for a chat, and he was always made welcome.

Laurie was by no stretch of the imagination a perfect pupil, his biggest problem was the fact that his work, although nearly always basically correct, was very untidy. He would often achieve the most difficult tasks with his hands (which would be essential for his future career). His hands were strong, but his book work was always untidy, no matter how hard he tried, it was a weakness which he was never to overcome. In a sense, throughout the whole of his life, the main tools of his trade were his hands, but his writing was always, and would remain his weakest subject.

Mr. Griffith, poor man, who was recognized as being an excellent English master, and also possessed a beautiful writing hand, despaired over Laurie. He even reached the point of threatening to cut out Laurie's football, believing that this would bring about an instant improvement, but it had no effect whatsoever. Mr.. Griffith loved the game too much to carry out his threat, especially after watching Laurie play. In spite of all his efforts and concentration to tidy up Laurie's writing, he was doomed to failure - it was always grubby, as he called it.

CHAPTER THIRTY

Christmas was only six weeks away. The Gilson family had arrived back from the Midlands during the summer, that would have been the summer of 1943 and Father was now firmly established once more in the fishing industry. Laurie had not been allowed to put to sea with his father until he had settled in at school.

There had been certain routines and chores that Laurie was expected to carry out as the only male member of the family still at school. These were duties that were essential to the success of the business and contributed to the finances. These duties came before sport or any other activities that Laurie might be interested in. He found that much more was demanded of him now than ever had been in the past. He quickly realized that he was going to have a very full life indeed, but his determination to be a fisherman never wavered.

It had been a family tradition to sell the smaller fish from each day's catch, direct to the housewives. The fish was cheap, and once Laurie got started, he soon worked up a good trade. This had to be carried out each evening after school.

Most Saturday mornings, if shell fish, such as shrimps, winkles and cockles were available, Laurie would take a barrow and do a round of the council estate. This covered a large area in the town and involved most of the morning and even going into the early part of Saturday afternoon. This never went down well especially when he knew the other boys were playing football, but these jobs still had to be done whether he liked it or not.

CHAPTER THIRTY ONE

It was four a.m. on a grey November morning, and this was to be Laurie's first trip out to haul the long lines which had been shot the day before. In one week he would celebrate his thirteenth birthday, but this was far from his mind at the moment. Naturally he had been out in the boats on previous occasions, but this was to be his first serious voyage to catch fish.

The cold North wind was numbing the exposed parts of his body, but he was much too full of excitement to notice.

At the moment, his father and partner Harry, were using a twenty foot open skiff in which to fish. Father did own a larger boat, but this he had chartered out to relations for the time being, and it would be some time before it would be returned. In any case the small boat suited their purposes for the type of fishing now being executed. It did have a fourteen horsepower Kelvin sleeve engine, but this was only used in emergencies, as petrol was still very short - the war still controlled and determined everything that went on.

The moment had arrived in Laurie's life when he would come face to face with reality. Now he was actually going to see what was expected of him in the future, if the sea was to be his calling.

Laurie had always known in his heart that it would be a tremendous challenge. From the stories he had read about the sea, he had no illusions of an easy life, the way he had chosen, demanded strength, stamina, courage and perseverance, if he was to fulfil even a part of his wild aspirations.

At Father's command, Laurie sat on the forward thwart (in layman's terms - seat) the rowlocks were shipped and the oars followed. Fortunately this was not the first time that Laurie had rowed a boat, but it was the first time with a boat of this size and twelve feet long oars, but it was not outside of his capability. He now began to realize just how strong a man his father was. They both had a grip on the oars, and with Laurie sitting down, he should have been in control. But as he pulled and Father pushed, his wrists were forced into the same action. He was being given a lesson on how to row correctly. The boat began to move forward and after a time Laurie automatically twisted the oars in his grasp.

When Father was satisfied that Laurie had the oars under control, he gave him a point to steer for and made himself look busy, helping Harry prepare the freshly baited lines that were to replace those that were about to be hauled, but he also kept a watchful eye on Laurie, who had a lot to learn when it came to handling a boat of this size. It would take many weeks of practice and much building of muscle before he could expect the boy to become even reasonably proficient. Not many people were capable of enduring the physical hardship and discomfort in this chosen way of life. Laurie was still very young, but it was the right age to start.

Father had never given a thought to Laurie ever becoming a fisherman, he had been the runt of the family, the last of the line, small of stature and always ill as a child, it was only in the last three years that he had begun to fill out and grow stronger. He still had his doubts that the boy could fit into this tough way of life, but Laurie's constant insistence that he intended to be a seaman had convinced Father that he should be given every chance.

The strong northerly wind which had not been so obvious under the shelter provided in close to shore, now began to make its presence felt.

Laurie was finding the boat much more difficult to handle as they came out into open water. As the movement increased, both oars became alive and were hell bent on doing different things, each had a mind of its own, causing Laurie real problems. He missed the water several times and nearly fell off the seat. Father and Harry laughed, telling him not to keep catching crabs (a nautical expression for missing a regular stroke). He was rocking the boat and making them feel seasick. They were enjoying his antics in attempting to keep the boat under control. Every now and then a white topped wave would shower Laurie with spray, this only added to his discomfort, but he stuck to the task in spite of the fact that he was beginning to tire.

Dawn was breaking in the eastern sky as Father took charge of the oars. They were approaching their objective. As night became day and shadows began to disappear, Harry sighted the marker dans that were anchored at each end of every two hundred hooks. The interesting part - the moment that Laurie had been waiting for all his life was about to begin. Very soon they would commence hauling the lines and hopefully fish would be coming aboard.

Laurie was so excited that he had forgotten about being tired and soaked to the skin but there was still a little while to wait. The ebb tide had not quite eased enough, there was a right time of tide to begin, otherwise the work ahead would be made harder. Very often in fishing, patience determined success or failure. Father and Harry were well aware of this and there remained as yet a full hour to dead low water.

Father explained to Laurie what his job would be when they started to haul. It was to be his pleasure gaffing and pulling the fish over the gunwale into the boat. Harry, standing on the stern, would be in charge and pulling on the lines, he was the one to decide when a fish was in a position to be gaffed and heaved aboard, (the gaff being a stick with a big hook on the end). Father was responsible for keeping the boat under control and in the correct position, it was his skill with the oars that could make life much easier for Harry, enough weight had to be kept on the lines to keep them coming aboard at a steady pace, if they came aboard too fast, fish might go under the hull of the boat and get fouled up, this could make all sorts of problems and might even mean the loss of a day's work, it was very much a team operation. Laurie waited with bated breath, he couldn't contain his eagerness and stood 'gaff in hand' ready to make a start. Laurie was amazed at how quiet it was, only the sound of the wind broke complete and utter silence. He looked from Harry standing aft, to his father resting on the oars in readiness forward, their faces lined, brown and weather beaten. There was little to choose between them, both in their late forties, neither had ever demanded much from life, working hard for everything they possessed. Laurie came out of his day dreaming. Father nodded to Harry, it was time to haul.

Conditions for hauling were not good, *Curlew*, which was the name given to the skiff, now lay more into wind than tide. As the Dan buoy line was passed from forward to aft, her stern gradually came round into what was left of the ebb tide, soon it would stop in the slack time that followed - they had work to do.

Harry was already laying back with all his weight on the anchor rope. Slowly it came clear of the muddy bottom, leaving about four fathom of rope to come before the anchor and hooks appeared.

Harry turned to Laurie with a grin on his wrinkled face. "Get ready, lad, I can feel 'em kicking" he said, the words were hardly out of his mouth when a writhing green backed cod came to the surface. It was a beauty, weighing all of twelve pounds. Laurie waited for Harry to give him a nod, then carefully using his gaff hooked the fish in its mouth and pulled it into the boat, with Father giving instructions all the time, Laurie cleared each fish from the line as it came up over the side. He was in his element when they kept on coming. The routine of gaffing, pulling aboard and clearing slowly became automatic, it was obvious from the start that it was going to be a very good days fishing. Water splashed about everywhere but cold wind and wet clothes were forgotten in the next two hours. There were eight lines to haul, and in between each line Laurie had to lift a floor board and bale out with a bucket, then a bowl, until the boat was clear of water. It was a thrilling experience for a boy on his first day at sea, and he enjoyed every minute of it.

The hauling of each set of lines had gone smoothly. Laurie was beginning to think that he could cope quite well, until Harry weighed the last anchor. He held a slack line in his hand, shouting to tell Laurie that the line must be broken somewhere. He warned him to be ready as the line was coming in fast and he could feel fish kicking.

Suddenly some twenty cod broke surface at the same time, it was like an aquarium, they all lay on top of the water, struggling to get free, but not one got away. Harry and Laurie worked in a frenzy to get the fish aboard, then lay back exhausted. Father rested on the oars grinning. It was a good day.

"That was bloody good" said Harry with a smile on his face. He took off his cap, wiping away the sweat and scratching his head at the same time, then seeing Father's frown, quickly added "sorry about the language Wal, but without little 'un we could have been in big trouble there." Harry was well aware that Father was against swearing, hence the quick apology.

Laurie stood up to his knees in cod, laughing, purely from the sheer joy of the battle.

What a catch. There must be almost a hundred fish, each weighing anything from seven to twenty pounds. Laurie turned to his father for guidance as to what happened next, but he had no time to ask a question. Father was pulling on the port oar and backing on the starboard oar at the same time, turning the *Curlew* round until she headed in an easterly direction. "Whenever you are ready Harry, you can start to pay away" he said, as the boat began to surge forward with the power of his stroke on the sturdy oars.

Harry picked up the first Dan buoy in his left hand holding

the anchor shoulder high with his right, he said "Ready when you are Wal."

Dan and anchor went over the side at the same time. The spare set of freshly baited hooks which had been prepared earlier went whipping overboard, the routine carried on, dan, anchor, line, dan, anchor line, and soon the eight sets of lines were shot. Sixteen Dan buoys bobbed away in the water giving one the impression that they were happy to be free and alive.

How he had accomplished the feat, Laurie could not work out at the time, but while hauling, Harry had managed to coil the lines back into their baths ready to go ashore and be re-baited for the following day. It was a work of art - Harry certainly knew his job. Tide had now begun to flow, and with the flood came more wind. *Curlew* was rolling heavily. After a short discussion, the decision was made to get into sheltered water as quickly as possible. Father opened the engine box, turned on the fuel and primed the plugs. The engine burst into life after several swings of the handle. Soon they were heading for smooth water where they would be able to lay in comfort, gutting and washing the fish, the cod would then be packed in boxes which were waiting on the quay. Although Laurie was only dressed in ordinary clothes, apart from an extra jersey and an old macintosh, he had hardly noticed the cold at all. The exertions of the day and the excitement involved, seemed to keep the blood circulating, but now as most of the work was completed, he felt drained of all energy and the bitter north wind penetrated deep into his body, chilling his very bones. He was starving hungry and needed a warm fire. For Laurie, his first day's fishing was over:

Curlew still had to be put on her mooring and stowed away, but Father, knowing that Laurie was bound to feel the after effects of such a day, sent him home. How pleased Laurie was that they lived so close to the sea.

CHAPTER THIRTY TWO

Laurie was to make three more trips long line fishing for cod that winter, they followed much the same pattern each time, apart from the occasional incident. One set of lines would be hauled, to be replaced by another. If the weather allowed and the fishing carried on for about ten weeks. The first day was one of the best catches, but generally speaking it was a good winter, the fish were plentiful due to the lack of boats fishing at that time. But there were so many other activities going on in the area.

There was always something interesting, something new apart from the fishing.

Barrage balloons hung like small air ships over the top of convoys to protect them from the enemy planes that were always on the prowl.

The ships would gather in their hundreds, waiting for Naval escorts, whose job it was to take and protect the merchant ships as they travelled all over the world. At times there would be so many ships, it would be a problem finding space to shoot the lines.

It became a regular and expected duty for the fishing boats to go alongside the ships, fish would be exchanged for chocolates and sugar, tinned milk, tobacco, or for that matter anything that was in short supply. The ships always appeared to have plenty, the seamen usually made a fuss of Laurie - he would be well stocked up with bars of chocolate, *Mars* and Milky Way, plus plenty of packets of boiled sweets. It was certainly a pleasure paying visits to the ships:

The pressure was gradually building up for the invasion of France. All was hustle and bustle as boats with stores dashed backwards and forwards between ships. Liberty boats ferried men to and from the shore, some going on leave, others possibly changing ships. The movement carried on day and night.

The streets of Laurie's home town were full of army trucks, tanks and equipment The people of the town entertained soldiers in their homes whenever possible.

Laurie thought it very strange at the time. All these troops and fighting machines, sailors and ships, yet no one knew where they were going, it certainly was a strange world.

CHAPTER THIRTY THREE

Life for Laurie was moving so fast now, he had so much to do that it was becoming a matter of fitting everything in.

His birthday passed quickly by and 1943 came to an end. It was Christmas, and Laurie, now in his fourteenth year lived a very full life. He always arrived at school a full hour before time because there was so much to do and so little time in which to do it. School life was gradually returning to some semblance of order after the initial disruption brought about by the war.

The whole school and each individual class were divided into four separate houses, every classroom was set out in the same way - four rows of double desks and each row represented a house - St. Davids, St. Andrews, St. Patricks and St. Georges.

A house master and assistant were appointed to each house. Once the division had been carried out, the boys themselves elected their own officers, the appointments had to be approved by the headmaster and staff.

A merit mark system was agreed, every activity that went on in the school came into the race for a shield that would be awarded at the end of each term, the top house being the one that had achieved the highest number of marks.

Having never taken part in anything like this before, it took quite a time for the boys to settle down to the new routine, it virtually changed their school life in just a matter of a few weeks. Apart from the odd rebel, who was soon brought into line by the rest, the challenge was accepted. As it included behaviour, one can imagine the drastic changes it brought about. Laurie had no problem as far as behaviour was concerned, his strict upbringing had instilled a code of conduct which he always tried to observe. He was also very popular with most of the teachers, this meant that he quickly became eligible for good conduct marks. This, combined with his sporting ability and mental arithmetic, plus the fact that his reading and spelling were above average, made him one of the highest merit mark earners in the school. He was in line to become a house officer in St. Georges!

To say that Laurie had a full life was an under statement. He played in the house football and cricket teams and hoped soon to play for the school.

Even so, with all these demands on his time, he went to sea whenever the chance came along. He would also meet his father when he came home from fishing in order to get aboard *Curlew*. He loved to row the big skiff off to her moorings and stow away the gear. Messing about in boats was not only good fun, it was also his future. About this, there was never any doubt in his mind. Father owned a small dinghy called *The Titch*. She was about ten feet long and five feet wide, built like a little tub, she was used just for getting off to *Curlew's* mooring. When not in use *The Titch* was pulled up on the quay and chained to a post.

The Titch had been built with what is known a Transom stern. This meant that the back end was more or less square, and in the centre a scull hole had been cut. Laurie had often watched Harry propel *The Titch* with one oar resting in the scull hole, then using a twisting wrist movement, with the oar blade under water astern, he was able to force the Dingy forward at a considerable speed.

Laurie was determined to master this way of sculling. It took him a long time to master the art of turning his wrist as he moved the oar from side to side, but once he got the knack it became second nature. The more he practised, the more skilful he grew, until even using only one hand, he could move the little boat along at quite a fair lick.

On one particular day, when several people stood watching

from the quay, Laurie decided to show off his skills. Using all the power he could muster, and putting on a grand display of sculling, he failed to realize just how fast he was travelling. The first warning of danger was a loud crunch as he ran headfirst into another boat that was moored in close to the shore.

Unfortunately for Laurie, just at that precise moment Father walked onto the quay - he witnessed the whole tragedy.

Luckily, the boat didn't sink, but enough damage was done to give Father almost a whole day's work, carrying out repairs.

Laurie suffered the inevitable consequences of his foolhardy showing off. One good hiding and no sculling for six long weeks. It was no more than he deserved, but he thought differently at the time.

The winter was nearly over and Laurie was anxious for the spring of 1944 to arrive. He had heard many tales of skate fishing in the shallow waters along the south coast. His father, grandfather and great grandfather had taken part in this fishery for generations, and by all accounts, it was a very competitive business. More than one method was used for catching these thorn backed fish and all these different types of fishing Laurie was determined to learn.

After Christmas, he moved into Mr. Jones' class, he was now in the top form of Southchurch Hall School, and also at the commencement of his last year.

Laurie was a little disappointed that Mr. Jones had not been appointed housemaster of St. Georges, but after all the miraculous things that had happened since those bad old days, when he had been afraid of school, perhaps that was asking too much. He had one year to go, and the whole time was to be spent with his favourite teacher, Laurie was content

The headmaster informed everyone at assembly (the first after Christmas) that elections for house officers would take place during the week. There would be four to each house, making sixteen in all. These would take on the responsibility of school prefects, and with the masters, would then vote for a school captain. The headmaster went on to explain "House Captains and Officers will be announced at assembly next Monday, there will then be a meeting in my study at four p.m. that same afternoon for masters and house officers, the new School Captain will be appointed at a special assembly on Tuesday, that is the following morning."

There was a buzz of excitement throughout the whole school, it was a new beginning, a sort of return to democratic rule. Each boy in some small way had a part to play in running his own life. The war had yet to go on for another year and a half, but a gesture from an excellent and thoughtful headmaster, brought a change of attitude into lots of boys lives.

The elections went on all that week, lessons continued as normal, but the atmosphere was changed, because every day a group of boys marched into one particular room to cast their vote. As the week came to an end, there was much speculation and joke betting on who would come out on top. If nothing else, the election had certainly stirred up a whole new interest.

At four p.m. on the Friday evening, the boys went home, none the wiser as to the outcome. For this, they would have to wait until Monday morning's assembly.

Laurie had mixed feelings about the elections. He thought it was a great thing for the school. It also occurred to him that he could become a house officer, perhaps football or cricket captain. After all, he did play in both teams, but he was not unduly concerned, most of the positions would go to boys who were his friends, so there was nothing for him to worry about. He looked forward to Monday assembly, with keen interest. Laurie had a very special friend named David Jones. David was also a good all round sportsman. Clean and tidy in his work, very competent in his lessons, in Laurie's opinion David stood a good chance of becoming School Captain, but as he was in St. Davids house, he was just another member of the opposition.

Laurie had his normal busy weekend. He still had to carry

out all his chores before going off to sport on Saturday, while Sunday had always been a day for church in the Gilson family.

Monday morning soon came round. Laurie as usual arrived early to find the playground crowded. He had never before seen so many boys waiting for school to begin, it showed the keen interest caused by so many fresh activities, especially the elections.

He made his way down to where most of his close friends would soon be involved in a game of football. It was an unusual game, inasmuch as no one ever asked which side they were to play on. There could be as many as one hundred and fifty boys all playing in the same game, but each boy knew which was his side.

The air raid shelters acted as goal posts, these were shaped like a wedge, being ten feet high at the north end, but only one foot high at the south end. This made a funny shaped goal, but the game had almost become a ritual. The teachers came and joined in and even they knew which was their side. The teams never had a half-time, or turned round to change ends, even if the game went on for three hours, which it sometimes did.

On this particular morning, many groups stood around talking, not quite so many players were taking part, but even so there were enough to make for a very hectic game of football.

Just for the moment Laurie had forgotten about the elections, he was somewhere in the thick of the fray, nothing else registered while he was playing football, the importance of the morning had gone, until the whistle went blasting across all other noises to bring him back to reality - it was time for school to start.

The boys filed into their classes for the register to be called, after this they marched in line to assembly.

First into the hall were the younger boys, who stood at the front. Class followed class until the hall was full.

Then came the teachers, who, for the first time since Laurie joined the school, were all present - they sat on the platform.

Mr. Jones, being head teacher, called the boys to order. They then stood in silence, waiting for the headmaster.

Mr. Haxall entered from the back of the Hall, walking slowly down the centre aisle between each block of boys. Taking his place on the platform, he started assembly. Perhaps the best way to describe Laurie's singing, would be lusty, it was a loud noise. Mr. Haxall had chosen one of Laurie's favourite songs for the start of assembly this morning - 'And did those feet in ancient times walk upon England's mountains green'. He knew it was a song the boys enjoyed singing. The patriotic words rang out loud and clear for the special occasion and Laurie was proud that he belonged to this school.

As the sound echoed through the old hall, his mind began to wander back over the past, the mention of England's green mountains took him back to the days of the canal barges and all those things that had happened in his early life in the Midlands.

He often thought about Rita - it was more than possible that she would be in college now, with her tremendous ability, Laurie was certain she would succeed, no matter what happened. The natural talents for anything she attempted to do, were sure to make her a winner.

Laurie came back to the present and reality. Mr. Haxall was reading routine prayers in a quiet voice. There was absolute silence over the whole school, apart from the headmaster's steady, almost musical chant. When he had finished all the boys said 'Amen,' and waited.

Mr. Haxall began to speak. "I expect the assembly to take an hour, there are some important announcements, and I also want to speak about the future of our school.

There is one sad duty I have to carry out and that will be done straight away.

Unfortunately, Mrs. Clark, who has been with us more than three years, is going to retire. This is a lady who has devoted all her life to the teaching of boys all over the country, and her service will be sadly missed. A retirement and presentation ceremony will take place at next week's assembly." There was a buzz of whispers all around the Hall. Mrs. Clark was not one of the most popular teachers, but there would be many who had a lot to thank her for.

Laurie smiled to himself as he remembered the constant battles he had fought with her over the years, but they were now good friends. Yes, he would miss her.

The headmaster waited for the whispers to die away, then continued.

"I have been headmaster of this school for a very long time now. The last few years of war have not helped to make the position an easy one, but the times are changing, we are entering a new era. We are going to win the war!" There were cheers from the boys. "And today marks a fresh start in the life of our school," (more cheers). "From today you will help run the school. I would not attempt to carry out this change unless I was sure that the boys were capable and willing to back the teachers and myself. I consider you to be one of the best groups of boys I have ever had the pleasure of working with. My staff are first class, that goes without saying. I know they will back me one hundred percent" - this brought more cheers from the boys.

"Last week, as you all know, elections were held in the school. From those election: we now have sixteen house officers. Shortly Mr. Jones, my head teacher, will read out the names of those elected. Just remember, you have put these boys in office, I shall expect everyone to give them full support."

The headmaster stood to one side of the table, behind which all fifteen masters sat in a semi-circle. Mr. Jones stood up and moved forward, a large black book held in his hands. He waited for the clapping and cheering to stop. When he started to speak, you could have heard a pin drop. There was an excited, almost breathless hush.

"The Patron Saint of England being St. George, that house will be left until last," Mr. Jones began. "Other than that they are to be announced in alphabetical order. St. Andrew, Cricket Captain, Bob Ross" - a cheer went up from St. Andrews house. "Football Captain, Jimmy Sayer" - an even bigger cheer from the boys. "House Vice Captain, Les Yates. House Captain, Tom Yates." The boys went mad, Laurie was not surprised at the selection of the Yates brothers as Captain and Vice Captain. Both played in the school football and cricket teams. They were twins and stood six feet tall and big with it. Laurie was glad they were his friends, at least nobody would step out of line in St. Andrews House.

All four boys went up on the platform and were congratulated, first by the headmaster and, then Mr. Jones, after that shaking hands with each teacher in turn. The members of their house cheered and clapped the whole time. It was fully five minutes before order could be restored.

The headmaster had been right - it was going to be a long assembly!

"St. Davids." Mr. Jones continued, and the appointments were made. There were quite a few surprises, but when it came to the moment for House Captain to be announced, Laurie looked across at his best friend, David Jones - surely he had to be Captain of St. Davids. No one in the House could possibly compete with him for honours. Mr. Jones hesitated, St. Davids was his own house. "I am very pleased to have as my own house Captain, David Jones." This was the biggest cheer so far. Laurie was doing something which was most unusual for him, he was jumping up and down with joy and shouting his approval. While David Jones was on the platform, shaking hands all round, Laurie's mind began to wander again. They had been friends from the day they had first joined Southchurch School together. David was one of the best. Even as he accepted all the congratulations, so thoroughly deserved, his face blushed the same colour as his fiery red hair. Laurie was convinced that David would now be School Captain. There could only be four candidates, it had to be one of the House Captains, and David was the ideal person.

Laurie had his heart set on being chosen Football Captain. He loved the game. To lead the House and then the school at football, would be a wonderful climax to his last year. The cheers had once more come to an end. Mr. Jones continued through the list of elected officers for St. Patricks. Once more the cheers filled the old hall. Laurie realized they were all his friends, in fact, on reflection, there was very little bad feeling in the whole school. Southchurch Hall School had an air of contentment about it, but this morning, that same air was charged with electricity.

Mr. Jones was speaking once again. "We now come to the last House, St. Georges. Laurie held his breath as the boys once again went silent.

"Cricket Captain, Richard Wyatt," this was welcomed with great gusto, he was without doubt the best cricketer in the school, his selection was no surprise. "Football Captain, Denis Flint," Laurie clapped, but he was unable to cheer, he was very disappointed, but he knew Don would make a good Captain. Mr. Jones continued."Vice Captain. Mike Wellman." Laurie's spirits soon lifted. He was well aware that St. Georges had possibly the strongest House with lots of hard workers to choose from, and at least he was sure to be in the team.

Mr. Jones had passed the black book to Mr. Haxall. The boys waited in silence - had something gone wrong, at the moment St. Georges lacked a Captain but the Headmaster appeared unperturbed. He stepped once more to the front of the platform.

Laurie, like all the other boys, was a little confused, but Mr. Haxall had started speaking once again.

"On Friday evening, after the results of the elections became known, a staff meeting was held in my study. It soon became obvious, because of the overwhelming majority of votes polled in favour of the four House Captains, that one of these officers would ultimately become Captain of the School. We therefore discussed the matter and came to the conclusion that only the Masters vote could effect the outcome. Bearing these and many other factors in mind, the vote was taken. We now have a School Captain, the decision was not unanimous, but conclusive. This has been a memorable morning for all present. I can think of no better way of making the occasion complete than to name our School. Captain immediately. Captain of St. Georges House and the School – Laurie Gilson".

Laurie was stunned, it must be one of his day dreams, there must have been some mistake. The thought that he might be House Captain had never occurred to him, but School Captain, it was impossible.

Hands were pushing and pulling Laurie from all sides. He tried to gather his scrambled mind. Mr. Haxall was calling for him to come to the platform, but he had no control over what was happening. His feet no longer touched the ground. The teachers and Mr. Haxall were coming closer, but not by his own efforts, he was being carried bodily towards the platform where the headmaster waited, a huge grin on his large jowled face. Mr. Jones could hardly contain the pleasure he obviously felt, and even Mrs. Clark had a broad smile on her face, as she kissed Laurie on the cheek. Laurie's hand was being pumped unceremoniously as the cheers rang through the school. To Laurie it was still an illusion, everything appeared through a haze. Fortunately the pandemonium continued for almost ten minutes, after he had been virtually thrown onto the platform. It gave Laurie time to pull his thoughts back to some semblance of order.

Tradition would demand some sort of speech. After such a reception, how could he reply when he felt so inadequate, so unready to accept the honour which had been bestowed on him. Laurie Gilson - School Captain. Impossible!

The noise subsided, they all waited as Laurie, now alone in the centre of the stage, searched for an opening quip, he must get rid of the tension.

"Who rigged the ballot? My two friends must have voted a hundred times each."

This produced a laugh and broke the ice for Laurie. It was a start.

Laurie went on to say "I am the most unlikely person to receive such a tremendous honour. Most of you will understand that there are so many reasons why the thought never crossed my mind. When I entered school this morning, any ambitions on my part were aimed at sport, but it was enough just to be involved at whatever level. Southchurch has come to mean so much to me. I would like to thank all the staff for their help and patience over a period of two and a half years spent at this school. I am aware it has caused some people much pain and frustration. Just five very short years ago, I hated and was afraid each time the bell or whistle went for school to commence. Then one day in the Midlands, a teacher arrived at the school I was attending, realized my ignorance, and decided to do something about it. He gave me a piece of paper on which was written a circle of numbers, and made me concentrate on them for weeks until I could add them up backwards or forward with my eyes closed. It is due entirely to that teacher I am standing here today - but I am not going to tell you his name."

There was a roar of laughter and cheers. Mr. Jones was famous for his circle of numbers. Well liked and respected by all, at that precise moment he appeared to be having problems blowing his nose.

Mr. Haxall, grinning and applauding, made him stand for the ovation.

Laurie finished his speech by saying "We have a great school, great teachers, its going to be a great year, a time in our lives we shall never forget." It certainly was!

As you can imagine, very little constructive work was carried out at school that day. Meetings were taking place in most of the classrooms throughout the afternoon. Assembly had lasted until lunchtime, it was as if a new energy had been injected into both boys and teachers alike. The old school had been given another lease of life, the building throbbed with the sense of challenge that now existed between the four houses. Each boy in his own way, determined that his house would be the best.

That is how it continued for the rest of a very exciting year. Laurie made many mistakes. He was very young for the authority which had been thrust on him, but in his rough straightforward way, handled the job reasonably well. What he lacked in brains was made up for with the vigorous effort that he put into being School Captain.

It took Laurie's family some time to get used to the idea. At first they thought he was pulling their legs, the dreamer of the family - School Captain. Not many years ago he held the record for escaping out of class at playtime. Laurie had been quite famous for his total disregard where school rules were concerned.

Today, Laurie was a very different person. Every month it was possible to see the change, both physically and mentally. He was always on the move and seldom slept for more than five hours a day, going to sea with his father whenever possible, selling fish round the town, yet still managing to keep up with football and gymnastics. All this, and his position at School Captain, made Laurie a most contented boy.

CHAPTER THIRTY FOUR

The bond of friendship with Mr. Jones grew stronger. As the days in his class rolled away, he confided in Laurie that this was the best bunch of boys he had ever taught, there were never any serious problems in the class, and not one shirker amongst forty boys.

In the new system, Mr. Haxall had incorporated a duty rota for house officers. A desk was installed outside the headmaster's study for the use of these officers. Any one entering or leaving the school would instantly be approached by one of the two boys always on duty. Laurie was often to be found at the desk, but there were certain lessons which he enjoyed so much, and could earn lots of points for his house.

When a lesson such as counting numbers was taking place, Laurie made a point of slipping into class. He reckoned on winning at least ten merit marks for each thirty minute lesson. Laurie got away with this for some considerable time, until Mr. Jones (who had twigged what he was up to) stood waiting for him to make an appearance, a handful of chalk at the ready. Laurie as usual, knocked at the classroom door and entered, only to be met by a barrage of chalk and shouts of laughter from his classmates, who knew what was coming. These were the types of incident that made school life so enjoyable in those last months at Southchurch.

The gap, which had always been so evident in Laurie's experience, between teachers and pupils, was blown away.

Mr. Jones set the seal as head teacher, his example was ever present. If the sun shone outside in the playground, he took every opportunity to lead the boys in a game of rounders. He had a wager with Laurie that he would never hit a tennis ball with a cricket stump, over the school roof, from the bottom of the playground, the prize being half a crown. Laurie never quite achieved this, but did manage to reach the roof and lose the ball, for which he received a traditional chase, and drubbing when caught. Mr. Jones also paid up.

In retrospect, those last months of Laurie's schooling proved to be some of the happiest and most contented, in what was to become a wonderfully eventful and adventurous life.

He played in both football and cricket teams, representing the school on many occasions. In fact, during the whole year, only one match was lost, and this to a college not far from Southchurch.

The boys and teachers had been discussing the possibility of finding some stronger opposition at football.

They had played and beaten all the local schools at their own level, so at Mr. Haxall suggestion, a fixture was arranged with the Baden College fifth year eleven. This would mean playing against sixteen year olds and presented quite a challenge.

The first game was played on the college ground, some ten weeks before Christmas. This would be the whole team's last term at school. They were determined and quite confident that they could retain their unbeaten record. Perhaps success had made them just a little bit too sure of themselves.

When the game was played, several of the masters and many of the boys turned out to watch.

It was a terrific contest and a real test of stamina for the younger team. They managed to hold out until the last fifteen minutes, in which time the college scored four goals. Southchurch did get one consolation goal in the closing seconds, but it was a very disappointed and tired team that trudged off the field that day, but they had learnt a valuable lesson, no one, however good, is invincible.

Laurie thoroughly enjoyed the game and pressed Mr. Baxter to try and arrange a return match before Christmas.

The headmaster promised he would do his best, although he thought perhaps the lads had bitten of a little more than they could chew.

However, the second game was fixed to take place just two weeks before the end of term. Mr. Haxall announced at assembly on the Monday morning that the return match had been arranged for the Friday afternoon and that the whole school were free to watch the game if they so wished. The news was greeted with a cheer. The boys wanted the chance to avenge that one defeat. It would be a great way to finish what had been a memorable year. Two days before the game, a discussion was being held in one of the classrooms, on team tactics, when Mr. Jones walked in. As always, the boys stood up to greet him, and invited him to join them, they would welcome his help.

Mr. Jones sat down and listened for a few minutes before offering any advice, then he asked "Why do you think the match was lost?"

Jimmy Sayer, who was team Captain and top goal scorer, replied that the forward line just failed to get going, which meant the defence were under pressure the whole time, he felt that in some ways he was to blame.

Mr. Jones agreed with the first part, but assured Jimmy that he was not to consider himself responsible. He went on to say "The reason the forward line failed, was because you were back, trying to help the defence most of the time, and that was a mistake. The College had one very strong and skilful player in their forward line, who was the cause of the trouble. If you wish to win the next game, this player has to be blotted out, he needs personal marking, one player, whose job will be to keep him out of the game.

Mr. Jones went on to say that although they had all played well in the first meeting, Laurie, who had played in the right wing position, was wasted, and would be better employed in the halfback line, trying to cut out the other side's most dangerous player. This would then leave Jimmy, the Captain, to concentrate on scoring goals.

The boys listened to the teacher and agreed they would give it a try.

On the great day, every master and practically the whole school turned up to watch. It was nearly Christmas and it was almost possible to smell the holiday spirit in the air.

As the teams came out onto the pitch, there was much cheering and loud shouts of encouragement for both sides. The College supporters were confident that these youngsters would not present any more problems than they had in the previous game, thinking that it was just a matter of how many goals they would win by.

They were in for quite a few surprises. Laurie revelled in the task of marking their best player and although his opponent towered over him by at least four inches. Laurie was now a small powerhouse, he had built himself a reputation of being fast and physical.

He clung to his adversary like a leech, completely putting him off his game.

The difference was unbelievable. Up in the forward line Jimmy Sayer was causing all sorts of problems for the college defence. At the half-time whistle he had scored two goals and Southchurch were two nil up.

In the second half, the pattern of play was much the same. Five minutes before the final whistle, Jimmy topped everything with another goal to make it three nil. Teachers and boys alike went mad, cheering themselves hoarse with the sheer joy of victory.

At assembly on the following Monday morning, Mr. Haxall, with a beaming smile on his face, congratulated the team on their victory. He considered that it was probably one of the best Christmas presents that anyone could have presented him with.

He called it a splendid way to end what had been a magnificent year for masters and boys alike, and one they could all be proud to have been a part of.

He then went on to make an announcement that was the supreme achievement, as far as Laurie was concerned. He knew that his house, St. Georges, had worked hard to win the house shield, but so had all the others, it was going to be close thing, and while Mr. Haxall went on, Laurie held his breath.

"It is my pleasing duty to present the winners of our merit mark competition, with the School Shield. In all my years at this school before the war, there was never such a close result, but it is my great honour and pleasure to present the shield to St. Georges Captain and Captain of Southchurch Hall School.- Laurie Gilson.

CHAPTER THIRTY FIVE

Laurie's school life was now complete, the rest of that last week was spent celebrating. Very little, if any constructive work was carried out, the whole time being taken up with parties and sporting competitions. It was indeed a very wonderful time.

Laurie was ready to leave school and seek to achieve his ambitions as a fisherman, this had always been his dream, but there was a very deep feeling of sadness as the last day came to an end.

All the boys in his class were leaving, and had made the rounds to every teacher to say goodbye, and were now converging on their own classroom for the last hour.

Mr. Jones sat at his desk, strangely quiet, as the number of boys and the noise increased accordingly. They sat around the room in groups, talking and laughing, one or two were clearing out their desks, ready to go home from school for the last time.

They were free to leave whenever they wanted to, but each one appeared reluctant to make the first move. Not one of the boys really wanted this special afternoon to end. The happy times they had enjoyed together in this room were nearly over.

Gradually they became quietly aware of the emotion that was filling the air around them. Reluctantly at last, two of the boys made their way toward the front and approached Mr. Jones. He stood up to meet them, both hands outstretched to hold them in that firm grip they all knew so well.

Others followed, each one was held in that intimate,

friendly embrace of farewell, before they left the room. Mr. Jones, taking his handkerchief out several times to blow his nose - he was obviously very moved.

Laurie and David Jones (Mr. Jones' House Captain) had waited till last. Their relationship with this man was more than one of teacher and pupil, much more.

The three of them stood, holding each other, and the tears ran unashamedly down their faces, before they parted.

CHAPTER THIRTY SIX

Laurie had now become a full time professional fisherman.

He continued to attend his old school, but this was in connection with gymnastics and only two evenings a week, that is if work would allow.

He visited Mr. Jones on many occasions and that special friendship was something he would always cherish, but the visits were only possible if the boats had fished the night tide. This would often leave Laurie free in the afternoon, after he had spent a couple of hours in bed.

Laurie not only survived, but flourished on just a few hours sleep each day. It was the middle of winter and very cold.

The main catch of the boats at this time was shrimps. As these were boiled on the boat, there was at least a certain amount of heat coming from the old fashioned coal fired copper. Even so, the freezing temperatures had to be experienced to be believed, but the thought that Laurie would ever work at any other job, never entered his mind.

To say that they were poorly equipped to protect themselves from the freezing conditions, would be an under statement.

There was money to be earned, but little to spare for luxuries like oilskins and sou'westers. Cheaply bought army capes and macs had to suffice, with as many old jumpers or jerseys underneath as one could manage to get on and still continue to move and work. It was two years before Laurie was able to afford a pair of Dunlop thigh boots to protect his legs from the cold and damp. But much was to happen before that great day.

Those first three months were the real testing time for Laurie

It was one thing to go out on the occasional fishing trip with his father, but something totally different to know that, come what may, day after day, week after week, fair weather or foul, the sea had to be faced, and it had so many different faces.

In spite of the hardships involved, the sea lost none of its magic for Laurie. Always the most exciting time was when the fish were coming aboard. It made not the slightest difference what type of gear was being used, the most important moment was when the fish hit the deck.

Some of the methods being used were very old fashioned, dating back to the days of the bible, when the disciples fished the sea of Galilee.

As spring came, and the water of the sea became warmer, so the type of gear changed to herald in a new season.

The same anchors and Dan buoys used for the long lines, came into operation again, but instead of lines between each anchor, there were nets, they were called peternets.

Each net was approximately seventy feet in length, and consisted of a straight piece of net, ten feet deep, but folded in half, then laced onto very thin, but strong lines. This meant, that between each anchor, there would be two equal stretches of line, one with corks on the top to make it lift, the other was weighted with small pieces of lead which carried it to the sea-bed. The fold of net billowed out behind the lines as the tide flowed through. This formed a long open letter box into which the tide carried any fish which happened to swim that way. Each end of the net was pulled into the shape of a pocket by threading a piece of twine through the end meshes and pulling them together to a depth of eighteen inches.

Sometimes when the water was very clear, the fish would see the net and swim along it, only to get caught in the pocket when it reached the end.

The nets were usually worked four in a set, and four sets to each boat, making sixteen nets in all, they could only be used in shallow water, a maximum of seven feet.

All was prepared for the first day's peternet fishing, the *Curlew* was ready to go, anchors, dans and nets aboard and waiting.

It was about six a.m. and a beautiful spring morning with just a very light southerly wind.

The sun, big, bright and golden red, had just cleared the horizon. It held all the promise of being a lovely day.

They were heading for a well known fishing ground, close in under the shelter of the Kent coast.

The area was famous for its prolific skate catches, but as this was the first trip of the season, nothing was guaranteed. The nets had to be laid on (as it was called) and it was going to take about one hour and forty minutes to get there.

The war was still in progress, but everyone was confident it would not last much longer. Laurie was helping with the preparation of the nets, but always on the alert for anything new, just happened to glance in the direction of the rising sun. Coming straight at them, out of a clear blue sky, was a plane which appeared to be on fire. Laurie pointed this out to his father, who said he had never seen anything quite like it before, but it could be one of those flying bombs which had been talked about on the radio.

The aircraft, though only small, made a loud throbbing noise, a buzzing sound like an angry bumble bee. It passed directly overhead, it was quite obviously heading for London.

Father's next remark was an unusual one for him, "The swines," he said, "it looks like something straight out of hell."

They followed the progress of that menacing, destructive object until it was out of sight. They could still just hear the noise of the engine, when suddenly it cut out. Just a short space of time passed, then there came a dull thud. Father shook his head in disgust, expressing the hope that it had landed harmlessly and that nobody had been injured.

This was the first of many Buzz bombs that passed over

them during the next few weeks, but the fishing continued and they became just another part of the scene.

All the nets had now been made ready, making a neat, but impressive stack on *Curlew's* stern. They were now tight in under the high cliffs of the Kent coast, almost to the point where Father would give the order for Laurie to let go anchor.

Laurie had been peternet fishing before he had left school, so he was quite familiar with the routine. Already he had prepared the anchor cable by running the bite of chain through a davit which was bolted to the stem of the vessel.

Father gave the word, *Curlew* was now almost at a standstill as the cable rattled through the davit. Laurie let six fathom run out, then checked it, taking a turn round the Samson post. He waited for it to come tight, then as the strain came on, he paid away another two fathom, avoiding any sharp snatch. There was only about nine feet of water under the vessel, nevertheless at this time of tide, the current flowed quite strong.

Having secured the cable, Laurie moved aft to where Father stood checking his landmarks. It was essential that the long span of nets be in exactly the right position and also laid in a correct line, for as the tide dropped and the water became more shallow, towards low water, the tide would change direction. If there were any skate in those shallow waters, this would be the time for them to move.

It was all a game of experience, timing and chance. Years of learning the trade passed down from father to son, and sometimes all the secret tricks were packed into just two or three hours fishing.

When eventually Father put his watch away and gave the signal to start shooting, the depth of water had dropped to a mere seven feet. One of the oars was marked for that purpose as this type of net was not designed for deeper water.

As usual, Father manned the oars, seating himself on the forward thwart. He made sure he was comfortable and that everything was ready - once the nets started to pay away, nothing must be allowed to stop them.

Father pulled the *Curlew's* head round, Laurie having weighed the anchor, and pulling strongly with the current, but just slightly across the full flow, shouted "Pay away Harry."

At a nod from Harry, Laurie let go the first Dan buoy and anchor, which was attached to the nets.

From the moment that first anchor gripped the sea bed, it was all go. It had always surprised Laurie just how fast the nets went overboard off the stern. At the end of each net he would be ready, anchor in hand, and every fourth net, two anchors and dans. No space was wasted, all four sets of gear had to be on what was recognized as the best ground, the fish seldom change their habits and that is where experience counts.

All of these tricks of the trade had to be learned by Laurie if he was to succeed in his ambitions for the future.

As the last anchor and dan went overboard, Father turned *Curlew* round into the tide, and just gently pulling on the oars, held her in a stationary position, at the same time asking Harry how they looked. "They look good to me Wal," Harry answered, "I think we have earned a cup of tea and a sandwich.

It was a glorious day, there was hardly a ripple of movement on the water, the wind having died away completely. With a good hour and a half to hauling time, there was breathing space to take stock of their surroundings.

Kent was a lovely county, with its mixture of hills and green fields. On a day such as this it was possible to see almost twenty miles of coastline, and none of its beauty was lost on Laurie, even if he was here to catch fish.

Every fifteen minutes he would pick up the oar which was marked, and tell Father how much the depth of water had decreased. The speed at which tide dropped was most important, and could quite easily determine a good days fishing or a bad day. The movement of the tide affected the colour of the water by stirring up the sand from the sea-bed and prevented the fish from seeing the nets and swimming along and round them.

So much depended on so many things, it was a very precarious way of making a living. But time was getting on, it would soon be all action, when they started to haul.

Laurie sounded the depth of water once again, then laid the oar inboard. There was only three feet of water underneath them, his keen eyes were riveted to an area at the back of the first dan.

Had he imagined it, or was there a movement? Sometimes if there was enough tide, fish would hit the slack net (which was called the lint) and laying across the tide, cause a ripple on the surface, this was known as a wake. Laurie thought he had seen a fish waking. He mentioned the fact to Father, who told him he was dreaming again. Father was not very hopeful about their chances today, he thought it might be a little bit early in the season for this particular piece of ground.

Laurie was now up on the thwart, pointing excitedly. He could see fish waking all along the line of nets.

Yes, there was no mistake, Laurie wasn't dreaming, both Father and Harry could see them now, and each had a broad grin on his face.

"Just give them another ten minutes and then we'll make a start," Father said, as he moved to take up his usual position at the oars.

In fact, the hauling was much the same routine as with the long lines on Laurie's first trip when he was still at school. Harry would be on the lines, Laurie would pull the lint of net aboard and also, hopefully, all the fish.

Harry had already lifted the first dan over the side, and now laid back with his weight finely balanced on the rope, see-sawing backwards and forwards until the anchor came clear of the sea-bed.

Laurie and Harry looked at each other, grinning with delight, it was like going into battle with the elements, as net lines cleared the water, and Laurie, grabbing hold of the first pocket, whooped with surprise as not only skate, but a fair number of plaice, came kicking over the side.

It was indeed a very good days fishing. Laurie was in amongst the fish and net, up to his neck, by the time all four sets of gear were back aboard.

While they were hauling, Laurie had been very busy, but not too busy to estimate that there must be close on one hundred and fifty skate and thirty stone of top quality plaice.

It had been five a.m. when Father and Laurie had awakened and left their beds that morning, one hour before highwater. It was now five minutes to dead low water, almost twelve noon. They had now been working seven hours and yet the day was only half way to being completed, there was still much to be done.

Nets had to be cleared of fish and washed thoroughly to prevent them from rotting. They were made of either twine cotton or hemp, the days of synthetic materials had not yet arrived. Then the plaice had to be gutted, while the preparation of the skate for marketing was a different operation altogether - they had to be cut up into several pieces, and it was quite a laborious task, as well as being very messy.

Laurie loved every minute of it, hard work presented no problems for him. He was filling out quickly and becoming more muscular every day. It was not clever or planned - his work trained him for his sporting life; his sporting life sharpened his movements and made him quicker, which all helped him as a fisherman - it was a perfect combination.

The moment every net was back on board *Curlew*, dismantling commenced, anchors and dans were separated from nets, which were then cleared of fish, washed and coiled into neat bundles, then stowed away. In fact, the whole process which had been carried out that morning while steaming out to the fishing grounds was reversed - the only difference now was that they had the fish to deal with.

CHAPTER THIRTY SEVEN

Curlew lay deep in the water, all the gear, plus fish, had left her with only about nine inches of free board all round.

When hauling the nets, a considerable amount of water always came aboard with them, this was unavoidable and had to be baled out immediately. The *Curlew* had to be as trim as possible if they were to make the journey back home in safety.

There were so many things to take into consideration, the southwest wind which had died away on the ebb tide, was now freshening on the flood.

In her present state of sea worthiness, the *Curlew* could be swamped by something as simple as a large ship's swell.

Father quite rightly decided that the safest way home, would be to keep under the lee of the land as long as possible, then cross the open water with the wind on *Curlew's* port quarter. Harry and Laurie concentrated on getting the fish gutted, cut up and washed, leaving the handling of the boat to Father.

As stated earlier, it was a messy business. There were fish guts, livers, intestines and gall bladders everywhere. The blood swilled about in the bottom of the little boat, but at that time, Laurie was too busy with the knife to notice, but he did think a great deal about it later on in his life.

Most of the boats which were being used for fishing around the south coast at that time, were old and made of wood. Several were lost at Dunkirk, and many others which had originally been built for sail, were converted to motor and used for all purposes.

Laurie's father had a boat such as this, she was built many

years before the war, as, what was then referred to, a pleasure boat.

In the days before the war, many thousands of visitors came down from London, just to go out for a sea trip. Laurie's father had the *Lady Doreen*, built specifically for this purpose. She was built after a fashion known as clinker. This meant that the wooden planks overlapped each other, as opposed to being carvel, which meant edge to edge.

When Father had first returned from the Midlands, he had set about converting the *Lady D*. It was a mammoth task for an unskilled man, and a standing joke for many years afterwards. The local fishermen would tell how he completed the job, using only a saw, hammer, knife, paint and putty. But in spite of the joke, many of them told Laurie in later years, how much they admired his father for the courage and determination he showed in tackling such a tremendous challenge. It gained him a lot of respect.

The *Lady D* was not really suitable for trawling. Lightly built and shallow drafted, she lacked grip and stability in the water, but in spite of this, she gave valiant service until replaced by something better, some years later.

About the same time as the war ended, Father had another boat built, called *The Boys*. The old *Curlew* had seen her best days, she was to be sold and *The Boys* was to take her place.

Laurie's older brothers were now returning from the Navy, giving Father something of a problem. There were now four of his sons, all wanting to be fishermen. It would have been even worse, but for the fact that Peter had decided that he would like to get some different experience, and had gone away to work on a salvage vessel. In fact, at that particular time, he was in Holland.

This left Father in the awkward situation that he had two small fishing vessels with which to earn a living for three grown-up sons, Laurie and himself. He had an uneasy feeling that there were going to be some difficult times ahead, and he was right. Father decided that the best approach for all their futures, was to concentrate on shrimps. Not all of the boys agreed with this policy, but at that time, Father's word was law. So that's how it all began. It was debatable whether it could have been called a good working arrangement or a good fighting arrangement: Certainly it was a hard time, also an unsettled one. It was obviously going to be an uphill struggle, of that, there was no doubt whatsoever.

In those early days after the war, everyone was trying to re-establish themselves. Laurie being the youngest boy of the family, got along well with all of his brothers. He was very pleased to see them safely back home, without suffering any serious injury.

Still barely fifteen, Laurie was even now looked on as the family pet, but with his enthusiasm for work and not having to make any of the decisions, he was popular with all concerned.

Ray the eldest brother, had a certain amount of fishing experience before the war, he was also a good engineer, so it was decided that Laurie would go to sea with him in the vessel named *The Boys*. Father would only go with them if they went peternet fishing in the summer. This left Bram the second eldest, who had seen a lot of action during the war, to work the *Lady D* with Henry, who had been on the canal.

Father would stay ashore most of the time, marketing the fish and shrimps, in order to try and make more money from the catch.

Laurie looked back on those days, as perhaps the hardest of all. He enjoyed working with Ray but *The Boys* was an open boat without protection or cover of any description, and it was a long hard winter.

Their boat was not big enough to carry a copper for cooking the shrimps, the only heat came from the engine silencer, on which they would warm tins of soup. This would be their only hot drink in many hours spent at sea. The shrimps they caught were trans-shipped to the *Lady D* for cooking.

Laurie would watch for the sun to come up each morning, praying that it would shine and bring a little warmth to their freezing existence.

Ray paid dearly, catching pneumonia, and being out of action for a very long time.

Even so, they both survived and came back for more. There was never any doubt in either of their minds as to their calling. The sea was in their blood.

At first there appeared to be some doubt, but as the spring came round once more, bringing new life, Ray regained his health and strength, and was soon back into the fishing.

They could not have known at the time, but it was going to be a bumper year for the peternet fishing. Spring came early, in spite of the ferociously cold winter. Very soon, in the shallow waters which surrounded Laurie's home town, there was an abundance of skate .

Father was back at sea with Ray and Laurie making up the crew of three.

Harry, who had worked with Father during the war, was taking things a bit easy. In fact, he had more or less retired from the more strenuous methods of fishing, to make way for the younger end, as he put it.

Laurie learned quite a lot from Reg. He was quickly becoming a good fisherman, and they had a great deal in common. It was often said that they also looked very much alike. But if Laurie had a special leaning towards any of his brothers, it was Bob The two of them could be found playing football together in any spare moments they had.

Bram had played for his ship's team in the Navy, and had also done a bit of boxing.

They both played for the same league club, in fact, all but one of the Gilson brothers, had at one time played in the same team.

Just at this particular time, Laurie was the youngest player actually playing in the senior league.

It was one of those few occasions when they all played in the same game, that something funny happened.

Going into spring, and being late in the season, it was one

of the last league matches, but Laurie's first for the senior team.

The opposition had a reputation for tough play, and there had been some doubt as to whether it was fair on Laurie for him to make his debut against them.

Laurie was not the least bit worried, and had been looking forward to the Saturday afternoon with great anticipation.

The game had gone well for Laurie his team were two goals up and they had only about five minutes left to the final whistle. Laurie was playing in the right wing position, against a big, bony, fierce looking man, who was almost at the end of his tether. He had been given the run around by this short but stocky youngster, who was once again coming at him, juggling the ball between his feet.

Laurie swayed his body to the left, giving his opponent the impression that he was going past him on the inside, but at the last moment changed direction, and with a twist of his body, went outside.

The big man was too late in trying to change direction and fell over on his right side, but as he fell he lashed out at Laurie with his left foot. The only way Laurie could avoid that lethal boot, was to dive forward into the air and land in a heap on the ground.

It could have been nasty, but he bounced back onto his feet unscathed. He turned on his opponent, intending to remonstrate about the tackle, but the sight that met his eyes made him smile, not only the referee was charging across the field after the poor chap, but also, close on his heels, were Laurie's brothers' plus the whole team.

This was all too much for his opponent, who turned and fled for the safety of the dressing rooms. Laurie thought to himself 'with a pack like that chasing me; I would have taken the same course of action.'

That was not quite the end of the story, the opposing club lodged a complaint with the league committee, that Laurie was not old enough or big enough to play in the senior league but this was promptly thrown out.

Laurie continued to play in that league at club level and also representative level, until he was forty six years old. He had a great soccer career and loved every minute of the time spent on a field, playing football.

CHAPTER THIRTY EIGHT

On the following Monday morning, Laurie was up very early, it was a case of being a sort of race for the Dogger Bank.

This was a bit of fun that was bandied about among fishermen, but it was indeed quite important to be first on the fishing ground, especially if it was peternet fishing.

As stated before, it was of the utmost importance to be in exactly the right spot, and the boat to anchor first on the grounds, automatically took first choice. This was an unwritten law.

Depending on which piece of ground one finished up working, could determine a good days fishing, a mediocre day, or, in fact, nothing at all. Laurie wanted to be first, that was why he was up early, taking in the nets which had been hung out to dry, and preparing *The Boys* for sea. The race was on. By the time Father and Ray arrived on the quay, the little boat was ready to go.

It was a fine morning with a light northwest wind, which was to their advantage. Father had decided that they would work along the north shores on this particular day, so unless the wind changed direction, they would be working in fairly calm waters.

To be working under the shelter of the land always gave Laurie a nice, safe, comfortable feeling inside. They had left the quay soon after three a.m., it was still dark, but Laurie was quite confident that they would be first on the grounds. There could be as many as six boats on the peternet fishing today, the numbers were gradually increasing, but it would be daylight before they would know for sure. The trip to the grounds would take nearly two hours and it should be light by the time they arrived.

Even now, as *The Boys* steamed through the darkness, Ray and Laurie were preparing each set of gear carefully, making sure that every time a net was laid on, each pair of end lines was fastened on the correct anchor.

All of this was, of course, now routine, but one had to remember that it was carried out in total darkness. It would be fatal if a mistake was made, and it had been known to happen. Light had begun to show in the eastern sky some time before they reached the grounds and the sun had just peeped over the horizon, as they let go anchor.

The Boys was definitely first boat on the grounds, but another arrived within ten minutes, and almost an hour later, when it was nearly time to shoot the nets, two more had arrived.

Laurie and Ray were well aware that Father had the choice of the best ground and they were at this moment anchored in perfect position to take advantage of it.

Second in turn would be the *Bona*, she was crewed by three brothers, all very experienced fishermen. Guy and Harry, the two youngest, were about ten years younger than Father and had both been in the Navy. Frank was nearer Father's age but suffered from a collapsed lung, this had prevented him from going to the war.

As was the custom, they came alongside for a cup of tea and a chat, which was very welcome. They were more fortunate than the Gilson insofar as they owned a bigger boat, all of thirty-five feet in length. The fishing was carried out in a small boat, but the cleaning out of the nets and the gutting of the fish was made so much easier on the larger vessel. They also had a galley for cooking.

Laurie with his enormous appetite, thought this was a great luxury. He was treated to a bacon sandwich and was quite content to lay back in the spacious cabin, with his feet up, eating his sandwich and drinking tea, dreaming of the day when he would own a boat like this one. He was not so happy ten minutes later when Father said to Frank (the eldest of the three brothers) "You can shoot away first Frank, then we can shoot away on your lower end." Frank accepted gratefully, "We'll get started now."

Father noted the look that Laurie gave him and stared back unblinking, daring him to say anything. Laurie said nothing, but the look said it all.

After shooting the nets had been completed, once again they all returned to the *Bona* for tea and sandwiches.

This was the first time Laurie had experienced the benefits of a much larger boat. When the nets were in the water, hopefully catching fish, they were able to return to a comfortable cabin and relax for an hour, sitting there listening to his elders tell yarns about the old days when they put to sea under canvas. Laurie soon forgot his anger at Father giving up the best ground. It seemed only minutes, but an hour and a half had passed when Father said "Its time we were having a look."

Both crews from the other two boats had joined them aboard the *Bona*, this made twelve in all crammed into the one cabin. It was a kind of communal atmosphere at sea, which was something quite new to Laurie. It was a pleasant occasion, one of those times which, in years to come, Laurie would look back and remember, and enjoy the memory. But for the moment, it was all forgotten, the men were back in the small boats, heading for the Dan buoys that marked each set of gear, there were sixty four nets shot in one continuous line across the tide. Each boat was heading for its own set of nets, and once more Laurie was up on the thwart, his razor sharp eyes scanning the water at the back of each dan. The tide was right, conditions were near enough perfect, and Laurie had the feeling that it was going to be a good days fishing.

As they came closer to the nets, Laurie's excitement began to mount, he could see wakes, lots of wakes and he was filled with the wonder of it all, behind the dans was absolutely boiling with skate, Laurie had never seen anything like it before.

That day almost two thousand skate were taken by the four boats. Laurie was content, but he made a mental note that the piece of ground Father had given up, yielded by far the most.

CHAPTER THIRTY NINE

Laurie had by this time become part of the establishment, as far as the fishing scene was concerned, in his home town.

As they all returned from the war, many who he could barely remember as a small boy, became good friends, and gradually he grew to like and respect most of them.

There were some great characters amongst them and almost every one had a nickname. It took Laurie some considerable time to learn them all and keep them in his memory.

One of the reasons he made so many friends was the way he was brought up. He had been taught always to respect his elders, and this important lesson he endeavoured to remember throughout his life, especially in his younger days.

He was not in contention with anyone because of his age, but the time when he would come into competition with other fishermen, was to come much sooner than he had imagined.

For the time being, everything about his life was good, lots of older fishermen played tricks on him, he was never slow to return the compliment, it all became fun and part of the joy he found in his work.

One of the nicest characters was part of a family combination of father and son. Old Charlie and young Charlie were the last in line of a fishing family that dated back generations. As old Charlie was now over sixty and young Charlie over forty, with no intention of changing his unmarried status or having children, it looked very much the case, that this would be the end of their line. Old Charlie was one of the great practical jokers, but he was also very generous. Whenever he called

Laurie over to speak to him, which he often did, Laurie never knew whether to expect something nice or nasty, but always when old Charlie called, his right hand would be round behind him, where it could not be seen.

One morning, when Laurie arrived on the quay, old Charlie was coming up the steps, having just left his boat. He had obviously seen Laurie coming and was ready and waiting for him. "Oh Lol," he called, in a singing voice, "I have something for you."

Laurie walked forward smiling, it could be a *Mars* bar, it might be a chocolate bar which Charlie had exchanged for fish from one of the many ships which were anchored off shore, but it was neither of these things, in fact, it was something quite different.

Suddenly Charlie's hand came from behind his back, and splosh, a large jellyfish landed in Laurie's ear. He staggered back, taken completely by surprise, while old Charlie doubled up with laughter. Meanwhile Laurie, after he had recovered from the attack, made a dash for the water and washed the slime off his face. By the time he came back up the steps, grinning broadly, old Charlie was well on his way along the quay, turning round and waving to Laurie as he disappeared round the corner.

Some days went by before the chance came for Laurie to get his revenge. The peternet fishing was in full swing and a regular pattern of working had developed.

Each day when the nets had been shot, all the boat crews would gather aboard *Bona* for a cup of tea and a chin-wag. It became such a regular occasion that Laurie had come to look forward to it. Old Charlie and son were nearly always in attendance, they also worked the peternets. Laurie was alert at all times when they were aboard the *Bona*, he intended having his revenge at the first opportunity. His chance came one day after the chin-wag and all the crews were preparing to go and haul the nets.

None of the boats had toilets at that time, and old Charlie

had a need to relieve himself. As was the custom, he went up into the bows, which was jokingly known as the pup deck, in order to carry out his ablutions. Having carried out his mission, he was standing with knees bent and his back to the crews, busy pulling up his long underpants, trousers gaping below his knees. This had not gone unnoticed by Laurie who was ready with a soggy spawn-filled starfish which he had found in the *Bona's* scuppers. Watched by the grinning crews, who knew of the good natured feud that went on between them. Laurie crept silently forward, placing the soggy mass in those gaping trousers, and quickly retreated. Old Charlie noticed nothing amiss when he pulled up his trousers and fastened his belt, the thickness of his underclothes and pants cushioned the mucky mess and his thigh boots stopped it slipping down. He turned and walked aft, thinking all was well.

They climbed into the small boats, some finding it difficult to conceal their amusement. Old Charlie climbed aboard his own skiff, moved forward intending to ship the rowlocks, and sat down. The result was electrifying, he leapt into the air with a loud roar and at the same time grabbing the back seat of his trousers.

The crews screamed with laughter, Father grinned broadly, and as they motored away from the Bona, Laurie waved cheerfully to old Charlie. He had taken his revenge!

CHAPTER FORTY

Although fairly strict routines and codes of conduct were adhered to by the successful full time fishermen, the job never became mundane. In most cases, the more experience a man gained, his respect for the sea would grow with it. Many lost life or limb simply because it was a very dangerous occupation, accidents were unavoidable. To take up the challenge of the sea was a risky business, and one not to be taken lightly. Routines and careful consideration for all the hazards were essential to stay alive. To know the sea was to understand its dangers.

One of the most important things in those early days was to understand the weather. At that time, there were no sophisticated long range weather forecasts to take into consideration. Day and night the men who went to sea made a study of the sky, closely and carefully making a mental picture of the sunrise and sunset, the direction of the wind and cloud patterns in the sky. A fisherman had to become a part of nature.

Laurie endeavoured to take in and learn all these lessons which were to have so much effect on his future.

The peternet fishing continued to be very good that spring and carried on well into the summer. Not every day was good, but there were not many bad ones.

As spring turned into early summer and the water temperature rose, so the green weed began to grow and the jellyfish increased in numbers and size.

Sometimes the nets would be blown out with these

unwanted intruders into the fishing, it usually meant a lot less fish and a lot more work, it brought discomfort and danger as well. Some of the jellyfish were enormous, when swimming in the water they appeared to be about twenty inches across. The whole of the centre of these larger types, was one mass of brown slime. The fishermen called them snotties, they carried a powerful sting and the irritation afterwards often unbearable. To scratch the stinging flesh was disastrous and meant agony for the rest of the day, the pain would often last many hours and the only relief was to douse the affected parts in as much water as possible and try to ignore the fact that the pain was there, the more it was touched, the worse it became.

Laurie had seen all of these problems and the discomfort that came from them, while he was still at school. At that time he was made to stand clear and not get involved, but now he was one of the crew and working, it had to be dealt with.

On this particular day, as they steamed towards the dans, Laurie was standing up on the stern as usual, trying to see if there were any fish waking, but all he could see was a large white mark behind each net. His heart sank, as he realised that the nets were full of green weed, if they were, it was doubtful that there would be many fish.

As they came up close to the dans, Laurie could see some wakes along the nets, but they were lumpy, not a bit like the mark made by a skate. He turned to call Father's attention to this, but there was no need. "Snotties" said brother Ray, "lots of snotties!." "Haul immediately" said Father, almost running to his normal position at the oars, "it looks like big trouble!"

Ray pulled on the dan rope, lifting the first anchor from the sea-bed, lines draped with weed, looking like Christmas decorations, came up out of the water, then the nets, choked with weed, and in each net several horrible looking snotties. They were indeed in big trouble.

The sheer weight of soggy weed and water on the lines, was making Ray pull hard, straining his muscles to their limit. Laurie grabbed the lint, relieving him of as much strain as possible, by pulling slightly ahead of him.

Under normal circumstances, both of them would have been shaking the lines and net in order to get rid of as much weed as possible, but the presence of the snotties prevented this. The slime was everywhere. Each time a whole one was about to come aboard, Ray would drop the lead line, leaving Laurie free to roll the large ugly jellyfish out of the net and back into the water, but the horrible slime remained.

The slow backbreaking task of hauling took well over an hour, at the end of which they lay back exhausted, wanting to scratch all over, but this was the one thing they dare not do. So far they had managed to keep the slime out of their eyes. This was more important than anything else. If the slime got into a man's eyes, it could quite easily drive him mad.

That day was a long, hard, uncomfortable one, which seemed to go on for ever. At the finish, all they had to show for it was twelve skate, aching muscles, and skin that irritated and burned like a fever. A day not to be forgotten, however hard one tried. After a family consultation, Father decided on the day following the calamitous episode with the weed and snotties, that a change of ground must be sought, even if only for the purpose of cleaning the nets. After such a day, the normal procedure would be to hang the nets out on the quay and leave them several days to dry, it would then be possible to shake out most of the rubbish, but they could not afford to wait for this to happen. The weather was holding good and they must make the most of the opportunities that were available to them.

Father suggested that the ground was almost sure to be clean on one part of the Kent coast which was not often fished. It was a little further away than usual but had a reputation for having a clean sandy bottom or sea-bed.

High water being at six o'clock that morning, they mustered about an hour before.

By the time *The Boys* cast off from the quay and headed for the fishing grounds, it was almost high water. If all went well, it would take just under three hours to reach the grounds. Much more care than normal had to be taken with laying the nets on, the bulk of weed still entwined in the meshes, meant that each set of four would have to be shot separately, there not being enough room on the stern for more than four nets at a time. Once again it was a lovely morning, not many miles had been covered, but already warm sunshine had spread its golden rays on the calm waters. Laurie took in the stillness and beauty of it all, as they worked, and in spite of the fact that they all ached from the strain of the previous day, he was filled with a sense of joy at being alive.

The exercise involved in preparing the nets was gradually loosening up their muscles. All went well and they were within three miles of the area to be fished, when suddenly the engine just cut out. Ray quickly removed the engine cover, and after a brief examination, announced that she was seized solid. The moment the engine had stopped, Laurie had shipped the oars and rowlocks and was now pulling hard towards their objective. Father and Ray were standing aft, having a discussion as to what procedure should be followed. There were no other boats in sight, so there was no possibility of getting a tow, either to the grounds where they had intended to fish, or indeed, back home again, which would be the ultimate goal.

The question on which they had now to make a decision was, should they continue on and row the remaining couple of miles, and fish, taking the chance that the weather would hold and allow them to row the twenty miles home later in the day, or anchor until the hardest of the tide had finished, then make tracks for home, without fishing at all.

Laurie was well aware what the discussion was about, increasing his stroke accordingly, the thought of going all that distance back home without fishing, was unthinkable.

Ray looked forward to where Laurie was now pulling on the oars like someone possessed, and smiled. "Looks like we are going to fish," he said, turning to Father, "lets try and get a day's work first, then we will worry about getting home later." So they carried on, with the tide behind them they soon covered the remaining distance to the designated spot, immediately shooting the nets which had been made ready. A second set was then prepared and shot, then another, making twelve in all.

"I think we had better let that do, for today," said Father, "with only an hour to low water, we must give ourselves thirty minutes to haul."

They were in an area where there was little slack water, the tide would continue to move anti-clockwise until it had turned full circle. The nets had to be back aboard and the hauling completed before the tide came up along the three sets of gear, if not, they would turn inside out and any fish that were in them, lost.

Laurie was keeping his fingers crossed, that there would be some skate, it was unusual to catch much else on this particular piece of ground, but it did have a reputation for yielding some very big fish, not only would they make good prices, but they also created such a disturbance in the nets, that it also helped to clean out the weed.

Laurie was watching for wakes, and his father knew what he was looking for. He too was looking along the line of nets, but for a different reason, he was watching for the tide turning.

Father put his hand on Laurie's shoulder and said "Don't be too disappointed if they don't show themselves son, we still have four feet of water underneath us and these big fish are inclined to sand up like an anchor if there's not much tide, but it's time we started hauling."

As *The Boys* stern came round and Ray put his weight on the dan rope, Laurie experienced that same excitement that always came to him - the thrill of seeing the first fish of the day come aboard, but as the anchor came clear of the water, the pocket of the net hung straight down. Something was wrong:

"Pull, Lol," Reg shouted, "there's a big one in the pocket."

Laurie didn't need telling twice. He stood up on the thwart, carefully balanced and flexing his muscles, pulled with all his might.

The net came away from the sea-bed with a soft sucking noise, and out of the water, alongside the boat, was the biggest skate Laurie had ever seen. He nearly fell overboard in his excitement, it took most of his strength to pull the enormous fish aboard.

Several feet along the net and the same thing happened again and again. Each time it took all the weight that Laurie could muster to pull the fish out of the sand. It was just as well Father had decided to shoot only twelve nets. They were averaging thirteen skate per net, if they kept up that average, they would have in excess of one hundred and fifty fish, each one more than twice the normal weight they were used to catching. Even now, as the fish were still coming aboard, Father was considering all the possibilities of the next few hours. The little vessel was now very deep in the water, with some six inches of freeboard at the stern. There had been no available time while they were hauling, to bale out, as was normal procedure. This must be the first priority, stability was essential, they had twenty miles of open sea to cross, and at the moment it looked like it would have to be row all the way.

Laurie had just pulled the last fish over the side, the stern cockpit was now piled high with fish and nets. They topped Laurie by about twelve inches, but this was only because there was still a certain amount of weed in the gear, but they had cleaned up considerably He leaned back against the heap of nets, a big smile on his face, they had caught the fish they had hoped for, he was happy. But there was no time to waste, the floorboard specially made for baling out purposes, had to be lifted, and the water cleared from that area first. This would make room for the anchors to be stowed away. Laurie had already commenced baling, while Father and Reg were untying the net ends from the anchors. These operations took about ten minutes - they were then stowed away.

Father now began to feel a little more easy, at least *The Boys* was now at a reasonable level. He and Ray would now start clearing fish from the nets. Even as he was thinking, Laurie was shipping the oars and pulling in a westerly direction, which was the way home. There were certain things in their favour. The tide was now running southeast to northwest, the course home being west northwest by west, meant that at the moment the tide was coming from almost straight astern, and increasing in strength all the time, but in the next two hours, this would alter, the tide would gradually back round to an east and west direction. Before this happened, it was imperative that they were off the flats and into the channel, in order to pick up that westerly tide.

Father told Laurie to keep her heading northwest, Pulling as hard as he could, every second counted. Laurie needed no encouragement, he loved rowing and was already causing the oars to bend with the effort he was making. It was evidence to the speed at which his strength was developing, but the question remained, how long could he maintain this effort, it was certainly going to be a test of his physical fitness.

The Boys did carry a small mast and sail, but on a day like this, without a breath of wind, it was useless.

Father and Ray had a good three hours work ahead of them, just clearing the nets and cleaning the fish. Every now and again, while they were at work, Father would glance to where Laurie pulling away with great gusto was making the oars bend, and marvel that this was the same skinny little kid, who had not been expected to live.

Father himself was an excellent oarsman, and noted that there was very little waste of power in the lad's rowing. They were making good progress through the water, in spite of the fact that the boat was very heavily laden and difficult to handle. If Laurie was capable of keeping up his present stroke rate, by the time he and Ray were finished cleaning the fish, they would have picked up the strong east west tide, and be well on their way, but three hours was a long time for anyone to row an unladen skiff, let alone a fifteen year old boy with a boat as deep in the water as this one. Even so, Laurie made it!

Father and Ray had just finished cleaning the fish when they picked up the hardest of the tide, they also picked up another blessing which Laurie was sure Father had been praying for, a light north easterly wind. In a matter of minutes, Father and Ray had stepped the mast and the little main sail was set. This made a tremendous difference to the strain on the oars and Father was now able to give Laurie a hand, while Ray set about stripping the seized engine.

In all, it took them almost six hours to reach home. By that time, Ray had freed the seized engine and assured them that they would be ready for sea again the following morning. Just at that moment, Laurie could not decide whether that was a good thing or not, his back felt like it was going to break, and he doubted if he would be able to sit down for a week.

CHAPTER FORTY ONE

While all these things were taking place, Laurie had not forgotten Rita and his life in the Midlands. Those many pleasant hours spent in the company of the Denby family, and how much progress he had made in that time. Life on the canal, the fun, thrills and exciting events which took place, would always remain in his memory.

His mother often exchanged letters with both Mrs. Denby and Mrs. Conners, Laurie would always send his love and best wishes, but that life was now in the past - it had all been part of growing up.

Laurie now ran his own gymnastics class, but at the same time continued his training course, which he had entered some years before.

The class consisted of about twenty boys, mainly from his old school. Most of them were a little younger, but very enthusiastic about gymnastics. They had been given permission to hold the class in a church hall, attached to the church which Laurie attended on Sundays. It all worked very well.

One day, an old friend of the Gilson family, whose name was Harry West approached Laurie with a proposition. He had just returned from service in the Navy and was a keen scouter. He wanted to start a scout troop in the hall where Laurie held his gym class, and the church leaders were keen for this to happen, but the problem was, they both needed the hall at the same time.

Harry and Laurie discussed the matter, and it was suggested

that he would try to persuade the boys to join the scouts. Laurie had his doubts, they tended to be rather a rough and ready crowd, but much to his surprise, they all agreed. This was when Laurie's family named him 'King of the Kids.'

Harry now had himself a ready made scout troop, also a few problems in the bargain, but in a couple of months, by begging, borrowing and stealing, they all had uniforms of a sort.

Inauguration night turned into a riot. What with the moth-eaten uniforms of all shapes and sizes, flags being upside down, and about twenty different salutes, some of them not very nice, they all finished up in tears of laughter - but the job was done.

On the whole, it worked very well. Harry was a good sort, it was just as well he had been in the Navy, he needed all the experience he had gained. It was decided that one Sunday the troop would go out on their first camp. In order to get to the wood in which the camp was to be held, they had to take a short bus ride. Naturally, when they boarded the bus, there was a rush for the upstairs seats. What with the stamping of feet and singing, it was quite a noisy affair, to say the least. The conductor threatened to turn them off the bus for rowdy behaviour. By the time they reached their destination, Harry was very embarrassed, to say the least, and more than ready to get off.

Fires were not allowed in the wood in which they were to make camp, so it would all have to be make believe. They chose a site just clear of the main path which ran through the centre, and set up their one tent, which was of dubious origin, someone had found it! Once the tent had been erected, the four patrols were sent out to collect fuel for the mock fire. Harry and Laurie began to unpack the equipment from the two old kitbags they had brought with them, including the food and drink. By the time they had finished, the boys were arriving back with arms full of wood. The last patrol to arrive back, arrived with something Harry had not bargained for. They marched into camp bringing with them fifteen very attractive girl guides. It was very clear that they had already become good friends and intended to stay. Harry, not knowing just how to cope with this situation, turned to Laurie for assistance, but Laurie was much too busy talking to a very pretty girl with bubbly blond hair, and appeared quite happy with the situation.

Harry had no more time to consider what to do, he was too busy dealing with the guide mistress, who came marching up the path, looking for her lost guides.

Out of that first meeting between the scouts and guides, many friendships blossomed, lots of invitations to parties went backwards and forwards between the two groups of youngsters. They all agreed that the first camp was a great success. All, that is, except Harry, who, once he had managed to calm the fears of the guide mistress, soon had another entirely different problem to cope with. Three of the very young scouts, who, were to say the least, a bit of a handful, decided that it was a waste collecting all that firewood and not using it. They had piled it high at the back of the tent, the temptation proved just a bit too much for him, the match was struck and the sparks flew, in more ways than one direction.

Flames leapt up from behind the tent, they were close to six feet high when Harry first saw them, and by the time he had decided that he should try to do something about it, the old tent, which had come off the back of someone's lorry, was all part of the fire. All the guides and scouts cheered, poor Harry looked glum. He reckoned that at his first camp he had broken nearly every rule in the book.

Laurie was quite happy with the outcome of the campfire, Tina with the bubbly curls, became his regular girl friend for some time, in spite of the fact that she lived in a village five miles away.

CHAPTER FORTY TWO

Laurie was welcomed into Tina's home without question. Her mother and father were quite elderly, considering Tina was not yet fifteen years of age. They owned a little multi-purpose store in the village, and at that time would have been considered rather affluent people. Their house, which stood in its own ground next door, appeared almost new. The front garden was small and tidy, but at the rear was an enormous piece of land which consisted mainly of orchards, apples, pears and plums. Laurie was invited to help himself to the fruit and he was more than happy to oblige.

Tina attended a private school, actually in Laurie's home town, in fact only about a mile from where he lived, and just a two minute walk from his old school. She was a lovely, talented girl, and an excellent pianist. When Laurie did manage to get over to the village, he was quite content to relax in an armchair, listening to her play. It was a five mile bike ride either way, and usually after a full day at sea.

Tina was not one bit like Rita. Sometimes they would walk through the cornfields and out into the pastures where the cows grazed. Here Laurie told her stories about the sea, and they quite naturally held hands. Sometimes they would kiss, and turbulence rushed through Laurie's body. Her lips were soft and yielding. The warmth she created, whilst in his arms, was disturbing. But Laurie was more mature now, and his feelings under control. That was as far as it was allowed to progress. Deep down, both of them knew it was a lovely relationship, but not one that would last for ever.

CHAPTER FORTY THREE

The spring and summer peternet fishing was almost at an end. Jellyfish and green weed made it virtually impossible to work the grounds. Very soon now the nets would have to be thoroughly cleaned and made ready for the tanning pot, in order to preserve them for the next season.

Laurie was going to learn another very important lesson prior to this happening. Skate tended to swim around in the warm shallow water, shooting out their jacket protected young, and recuperating by feeding on the cockles which lay in abundance on the filthy weed covered sands. This carried on throughout the summer months.

During this period, the female skate became very thin and weak, needing all the food they could find, their main diet being cockles and crabs.

One very interesting feature of the reproduction cycle of these fish is that they are more or less identical to human beings, conceiving their young in much the same way, carrying very few eggs each year.

Just before all of these very interesting wonders of nature began to take place, Father decided that they would make one more trip. They set out on a pleasant morning in company with two other boats, obviously the skippers had the same intention, one last effort before changing to another type of fishing. Father had not expected that they would have company, but there was no hurry, all the boats had reduced their number of nets from sixteen to twelve, so there would be plenty of space for the three boats without racing. It was more than likely that the fish would be there, the question was, would they be able to catch them, because of the weed and snotty jellyfish. Even now, as they steamed through the water, the surface of the sea was covered with them. They spewed out of the bow-wave almost like a solid mass. The thought came to Laurie that if only they could colour them and make them sweet, their fortune would be made.

As usual the nets were laid on *The Boys* stern ready to shoot, and when they eventually reached the fishing grounds, everything was in readiness, they only had to wait for the right time. They had been last to arrive, this meant the other boats had first choice. They settled down with a sandwich and a cup of tea from a flask that Father had managed to acquire. The big boat called *Bona*, with all her luxury, was not at sea today.

Laurie sounded with the oar, and noted the time. Seven feet of water, right on the mark.

It would soon be time to shoot and there was already some movement aboard one of the other boats, but they were not in any great hurry.

There was one addition to the gear that they normally carried. A small steel triangle with net behind it called a telltale. Ever since they had arrived on the grounds, Father had been pulling it up and down from the sea bed on a piece of rope. Each time it came up, several strands of weed were on the rope, and much more in the net itself. Father shook it clean and lowered it to the bottom once more.

One hour passed. First one boat, then the others, had shot their nets, but Father just kept pulling the telltale up and down.

Laurie was getting a bit agitated, he dipped the oar, they were down to four feet of water, and although Reg appeared unconcerned, surely they would have to shoot the gear soon. Another ten minutes past, The other boats had started to haul their nets, something had to be very wrong, there was still almost an hour to low water, and they were hauling all of their nets as quickly as was humanly possible. Laurie could see that as soon as half of the gear was in the stern, they were so deep in the water, they were forced to haul the rest of the nets forward, in the bows.

Once again Father pulled up the little telltale, this time keeping it aboard. The green weed was less, but there was still a lot. He turned to Ray, "We'll go and speak to the others, if there are a few fish, then we might shoot for the last twenty minutes."

As they pulled alongside the boat nearest to them, Eddy, the skipper, shouted "I should think there must be a hundred fish Wal, but the gear is chock-a-block with dirt. Laurie could see that the boat was dangerously low in the water, Father asked if they needed any help, Eddy replied "No thanks all the same Wal, once we get the water out of her, we shall be alright, at least we've got a day's work."

Father shipped the oars and turning the skiff across and slightly into what was left of the tide, said, "Shoot away when you like Ray, it's now or never."

Laurie let go the first dan and anchor, Ray stood watching over the nets, making sure they ran clear, time was short; there was now a sense of urgency!. Two sets of gear had gone overboard and Laurie had just let go the first dan of the last set. As the anchor held and the last four nets began to fly off the stern, he glanced quickly back along the gear which had only been in the water a couple of minutes. He let go the next anchor, then looked again, excitement stirring inside him. There were wakes already, lots of them, even as they were shooting the nets, fish were hitting them and coming to the surface. Laurie let go the last anchor and dan, he turned to tell Father, but he had no need, Father had already seen. "Just ten minutes" he said, "then we will haul." There was barely time to unship the oars.

Father was true to his word, ten minutes had barely passed and they had started hauling. Laurie was laughing and shouting with excitement, Ray and Father were almost as bad, urging Laurie to pull the fish aboard more quickly and not to mess about, but knowing full well the effort he was having to put in, so that the skate would keep coming and not go underneath the boat's bottom. Thirty skate in the first net and the number increased as each net came up over the side, and they were cleaner than when they went overboard. They also had to haul six nets at each end of the boat, but it was all skate, well over six hundred in only twelve nets. What a catch!

Having caught so many fish, it was only possible for them to unfasten the anchors and stow them away, the water had been baled out, but even so the little boat was so deep in the water with fish, she was not seaworthy. They had to be very careful how they moved about.

There was no question of clearing the nets. As soon as they had done everything possible to make her stable, the engine was started and put in ahead. They dare not risk using any power, for fear of pulling her stern under water. It was going to be a long, slow journey home, with lots of work to do when they arrived. The nets had to be cleared and washed and the fish cleaned, washed and boxed. But Laurie couldn't have cared less, he never gave a thought to what would have happened if the boat had capsized. With all the excitement of having a boat full of fish, he had completely forgotten the fact that he was unable to swim, at that time. He had learned the lesson from Father, that patience is often well rewarded.

CHAPTER FORTY FOUR

While Father, Ray and Laurie were engaged in the peternet fishing, the *Lady D* had continued to catch shrimps, and keep the customers happy, as Father put it. However, this did not keep Henry and Bram happy. Shrimping was a rather boring type of fishing, when compared to most others, but it was all part of the family business and there was also lots of skill attached to it. They became good at the job despite the fact that the *Lady D* was inferior to most of the other boats involved in the fishery.

Once again, experience was most important and there was keen competition as to who could catch the most and the biggest. The art of cooking was also a decisive factor, when it came to selling the shrimps. All these skills had to be mastered.

Ray and Laurie, now that the peternet fishing was at an end had to prepare their own shrimp gear. This had been stored away for the last three months, it would now have to be taken out of storage, soaked, and rigged, ready for use.

The shrimp gear consisted of a twenty two feet long wooden beam. It was just a tree in its natural form, but with the bark stripped off. A ferrel, which looked like a top hat with the top knocked out, was then fitted to a small end, this had been specially made of steel, and to size. A sledge hammer was then used to drive the ferrel on to the beam end. The opposite end of the beam was cut square, it was then ready to receive the trawl heads which were also made of steel and very heavy. Two inch thick shoes, six inches wide, formed the bottom half of the trawl head. These held the trawl tight to the sea-bed, acting as skis on either side, the top half of the heads were made of a lighter material, usually two inch diameter, but still very strong and lifting the beam to a height of eighteen inches off the sea-bed, thus once again forming the letter box shape. The net headline would be pulled tight between the two heads, the foot line attached to a thick ground rope, which combed the sea-bed and lay in a half circle behind the heads when towed along.

The net was a simple basic small mesh trawl, 'V' shaped with top section called uppers, bottom section called grounds, and side panels known as gorings. In principle, everything which entered the letter box followed the shaped netting and finished up in the cod end, which was the narrow part at the back. All of this had to be soaked in the sea for at least two days before being used. Only one more thing was needed and that was the towing bridle, this was already aboard *The Boys*, waiting to be shackled on. Father's insistence that the financial security of the family depended on shrimp fishing, and must always take first priority, often met with considerable opposition from his sons.

It appeared to them that although the relationship that Father had built up with customers, was a good one, it quite often only worked in their favour, and not for the benefit of the family.

It was always obvious that when the two boats were concentrating on shrimp catching, money would be in very short supply, even when catches had been good. Monday and Tuesday they would fish for local trade and London market. This was never very successful, local demands were only limited, and it was not unusual for them to receive what was then known as a dead letter back from the market. This indicated that the shrimps had not been sold, and after suffering many hours of hardship and seemingly endless toil, the reward would be nothing. They only existed on the remaining four days of the week, salting down the shrimps and storing them in large containers. These were for the weekend trade, which was usually very good. The customers were wholesalers, who delivered all round the City of London and the surrounding area, often as many as five hundred gallon measures of shrimps would be sold to these dealers. It was this trade that Father depended on, but even this was not completely reliable. Hot weather or just general lack of demand, often resulted in shrimps which had been stored, having to be thrown away.

Laurie got the impression that the cards were always stacked in favour of the customers. It was inevitable that the last word was with them, but Father gave the orders, his word was still law and had to be obeyed.

CHAPTER FORTY FIVE

The Boys was now back in the shrimp fishing. Ray and Laurie got on well together and although Laurie was quite content, there was an added advantage with Ray being the eldest of the family. He would sometimes take the liberty of steaming away from the shrimp ground, contrary to Father's orders, and go looking for Dover soles and plaice. This all went towards making the job more interesting, but the sea never lacked interest, every day was different, and with each day came a new experience to be recorded in Laurie's memory.

Fishermen of that time, were ever on the alert for debris floating on the surface, or even partly submerged. So much shipping had been sunk on the south coast and in the English Channel, that when the wind was in certain directions, it was not unusual to see anything from a ship's lifeboat to a sailor's wallet, floating around in the water, and sad as it was, even a seaman's body.

The fishing still went on, whatever else happened, a living still had to be earned. Out of the many objects recovered, one was a watertight container, full of what the fishermen referred to as spewbags. These bags were given to passengers aboard ships if they suffered from sea sickness. There were several thousand bags in the container, and they were to come in very handy shortly after they were picked up from the sea.

It was now almost mid summer, and the *Lady D*, with her decks full of shrimps, was heading for home.

Bram had the old boiler fire roaring away, and was cooking the catch as fast as was possible. Fortunately the shrimps were nice and clean. There was very little rubbish to be picked out, this meant that they only had to be washed through a sieve and could then go straight into the boiler. He had plenty to keep him busy. *The Boys* was alongside as they slowly made their way towards the quay. Ray and Laurie were cleaning their own catch, but they all had to be cooked aboard the *Lady D*. When cooked, the shrimps changed colour, from a murky grey to a lovely golden brown. They looked delicious, Laurie was constantly being reprimanded for eating them. Spread out on the cool net along the port side of the *Lady D*, they made a very impressive sight to the crowds of people lining the Pier above. As the two small shrimp boats pulled alongside the quay, the smell of the old copper boiler and the cooking shrimps attracted even more people. Soon they were shouting down to the four brothers, wanting to buy.

As the tide was still quite low, it was a long way up from the boats to where all the willing customers were standing, and they would not be allowed down the slippery steps that was for certain.

An opportunity to serve so many customers for spot cash was too good to miss. After a short discussion, Laurie was despatched away up onto the Pier, with a bucket attached to a long piece of rope. He had to push his way through in order that he might line up with the boats below. Now that he was in position, Laurie was using his knees against the safety stanchions to stop himself being pushed off the Pier by the anxious customers. Meanwhile, down below, Bram was still busy cooking, every few minutes he would remove a small metal plate from the side of the old copper and blow vigorously. As a result of his efforts, a great cloud of soot would come out of the copper funnel , smothering the people up top, but they were not deterred. A loud cheer went up as they waved their hands in the air, trying to clear away the black smuts. Bram just looked up and grinned. Laurie now had the bucket going up and down like clockwork, the sixpences and shillings had begun to flow into his pocket, but there was a problem, they had run out of bags. It appeared that their little bonanza was going to be short lived, then Ray had a brainwave.

Turning to Henry, he asked what had happened to the spew bags. Ray soon had the casing undone and the bags up on deck. Once again the flow of the bucket got under way. Laurie was quite certain that the people had no idea what the bags were intended for, they were content that they had bought fresh shrimps straight from the boats. Bram continued with the cooking, Ray and Henry kept on filling the bags, Laurie pulled the bucket up and down at top speed and the people still continued to come. But now another problem had developed. Laurie had so much weight of silver in his trouser pockets, that his trousers began falling down around his knees. He was not going to give up for a little thing like that, so letting go of the rope for a moment, and trapping it under his foot, he hitched up his trousers and once again, wedging himself against the safety stanchion, continued to pull the bucket up and down, until at last, every customer had been satisfied. When he at last let go of the bucket rope and staggered down the steps of the Pier, his pockets were so full, he was certain that they were going to break. He stepped aboard the boats, laughing all over his face. Brother Bram, completely covered with soot, grinned at him, "I had a job keeping up with you at times," he said, playfully cuffing Laurie round the ear. "You had better go down below with that lot before it goes all over the deck." Laurie, clutching his trousers underneath his pockets, went down below to count the takings. While he was counting the money, brother Ray had a complaint from the harbour master concerning the mass of shrimp heads up on the Pier, but Laurie knew nothing about this. By the time he had come back up on deck, the boats had almost reached their moorings on Southend Fore-shore the copper fire was out and his brothers had almost cleared up and stowed away. They turned to him with a look of expectancy on their faces. "Well, how much?" Ray asked impatiently. "Well, it was a pity we didn't sell two more shilling bags," said Laurie, in sombre tones, and purposely keeping them waiting. "How much?" asked Bram, leaning towards Laurie and lifting his fist. "Thirty pounds, all but two shillings," said Laurie, standing back, enjoying the amazement on their faces. "Thirty pounds!" Ray repeated in disbelief, "that's a small fortune," and in those days, it was.

CHAPTER FORTY SIX

It was to be many years before most of the traces of war could be cleared from all coastal waters around the British Isles.

Henry and Bram continued to fish for shrimps in the *Lady D*. Ray and Laurie alternated between shrimp and peternet fishing, but it was a very hazardous business, to say the least. There were certain grounds which could be worked, where a mixture of shrimps and fish were available. Much of this ground was rough, with numerous wrecks which had never been marked in any way at all, not even during the war. Some of these wrecks were large ships, which had sunk after striking a mine. Several had broken in half with the force of the explosion, but even at highwater, much of the superstructure and masts stood out ominously, reminding fishermen of constant danger, which was ever present. Whether on the surface of the water or underneath on the sea-bed, problems created by this wreckage were very real.

Much of the rich fishing grounds lay off the coast of Kent, and had not been worked at all for most of the war years. On one patch, covering no more than four square miles, it was virtually a graveyard of ships, one being a whole Royal Navy destroyer. She had been blown up by an enemy mine, and her bridge stood out above the highwater mark, like a sentinel, warning all and sundry to keep well clear.

Whenever Laurie came close to this place, he always experienced an eerie sensation, he could never forget that his brother Bram had spent much of the war aboard a similar type of ship. These memories would not fade easily, if ever. But fish had to be caught, and the ground opened up once more. Many risks were taken and nets damaged in the continuing efforts to make the ground workable once more.

For Laurie, every day was a new adventure each time another haul was made, so many different objects would come up in the cod end, sometimes to be handled carefully and treated with great respect. There were many mines, bombs and explosive shells, lying on the sea-bed, just waiting for one of the boats towing a trawl, just waiting to create havoc.

Now and then an object would be recovered without doing serious damage, and sometimes it could be of some value, but more often than not, nets were badly torn, even lost completely. Such was the life of a fisherman in those very insecure days. Laurie learned his trade the hard way, through mistakes, hardship, and often very bitter experience. However much hard work was carried out in those early days after the war, the Gilson brothers fully realized, that without bigger boats and more power, they had no chance whatsoever of fulfilling their ambitions. So it was with considerable excitement and relief, that they received the news from Father, of the impending return of the *Reindeer*. This was the vessel Father had chartered out to the Osbourne brothers, Who had lost their boat (*The Renown*) at Dunkirk when she hit a mine. The *Reindeer* was thirty three feet in length and eleven feet wide, powered by a Kelvin diesel, and almost twice the power of the *Lady D*.

Because of her very sleek lines, she was reckoned to be one of the fastest sailing boats in the old cockle fleet. New vessels were now coming off the slipways, but to the Gilson brothers the return of the *Reindeer* was a tremendous step forward. For Ray and Laurie it meant that never again would they have to fish out a winter in an open boat. No longer would they run the risk of freezing to death, for want of a hot drink and a warm fire. The *Reindeer* had a large cabin, and by their standards, well equipped. At last they would be in a position to make progress. With the return of the *Reindeer*, Father came back to sea for a short period. Laurie became third hand and life was relatively easy for him. Although he spent most of his sea time aboard the *Reindeer*, it became routine practice for him to move from one boat to another, depending on which boat had the most work to do.

All gear up to this time was hand hauled. Once the bridle block was aboard, it became a race as to who managed to get his end of the net up on the surface first. Father was not allowed to pull on the bridle any more, and Laurie would almost bust his gut with the effort to get his end of the net up first, but somehow Ray always seemed to be just that little bit in front.

With the bigger boat at work, they now had much more flexibility. When shrimps were scarce in waters close to home, it was possible for them to push further out in search of better grounds, but of course, weather was always the deciding factor. On one such day, the two boats were fishing about a mile south of the sunken Navy destroyer. Fishing was good and also much more interesting because the catch was mixed. Each haul yielded about a stone of Dover soles, plus a basket of plaice, and one or two skate on top of the ten or fifteen gallons of shrimps each time. But the presence of a type of pipe weed on the ground, made it hard work cleaning the shrimps. There was also another alien specie adding to the discomfort, Fishermen called them flying crabs, they were fast and lethal. Tiny wings on the back legs, made them flyers. The brothers were used to handling the ordinary scavenger crabs, often the decks would be alive with them. Usually, the big old green, and red backs would crawl out of the shrimps and into the scuppers. If they were unable to get through, due to their size, they would wait until they were shovelled overboard later. But the flying crabs did not behave in this obliging fashion. They lay quietly, amongst the rest of the catch, with razor-sharp claws open and ready to grab at the first object within reach. If it happened to be a finger, the pressure was applied until the pincers came together and blood would flow.

Having three hands aboard *Reindeer*, made a great deal of difference. It meant that apart from when they were hauling, Laurie was able to concentrate on clearing rubbish and picking the shrimps clean. The fact that he was young, his fingers nimble, and his reflexes fast, pitting his wits and speed against the flying crabs became a sort of game, but a rather painful one if you lost. Laurie enjoyed all these challenges, it was part of the job, a way of life, and he loved it.

CHAPTER FORTY SEVEN

Reindeer steamed slowly towards *Lady D*. She had just hoisted her last haul aboard, It was a fair sized bag, but her decks had been cleared ready. Father was looking well pleased. They had made five hauls that day, to have everything ready as the cod end swung inboard, was some achievement.

Lady D was now only a few yards away. As the boats came closer together, Father could see at a glance that Henry and Bram were in rather a sorry state, He was not surprised, cleaning each haul while fishing on dirty ground like today, would have been a miracle with just the two of them.

The decks of the *Lady D* were full of uncleaned fish and rubbish, it appeared that Bram had a problem with the copper, and this had put them even further behind. He was not very happy, and had wanted to stop fishing for an hour, in order to take the copper apart and re-cement it. This operation had to be carried out every few weeks. If not, the circulation of air round the boiler was wrong, making it slow to boil. But Henry had refused to stop, the air was rather blue, to put it mildly. Working on instructions from Ray, Laurie jumped aboard *Lady D* as the two boats came alongside each other. Ray shouted, "If you are not clear by the time we get home, we'll come and give you a hand," and with that the two boats pulled apart. They had no way of contacting each other, except by shouting or prearranged signals. Most of the conversation had been lost in the wind which was now beginning to freshen, this was possibly just as well, because Bram was not in a very complimentary frame of mind.

Laurie jumped down into the hold with Bram, and making a space, set about clearing shrimps and fish from the rubbish. Not having to worry about the boiler, he soon began to make an impression on the great heap, and with Henry working at the other end, they soon started to get things under control. Bram was still fighting a battle with his boiler. It was cooking, but not fast enough. Every few minutes he would open the little door which was specifically for cleaning out soot, puff out his cheeks and blow with all his might. A great cloud of black smoke and large pieces of soot would come out of the long funnel, but he failed to make it boil any faster, and, by this time his face was almost black. Just to make matters worse, it started to rain, and Bram decided to put on his waterproof cape, Which, looking back, Laurie found somewhat difficult to describe. It was an ex-army camouflaged three quarter length shoulder cape, well, that is, it was once. One sleeve was missing, half of the left side had been torn off at the bottom, and to cap it all, there was a gaping hole in between the shoulder blades, all of twelve inches long. The hood had also disappeared. With his black face streaked by streams of sooty water, he looked like the devil incarnate ready to kill.

The *Lady D* had at that precise moment turned into the wind, which had now become more than fresh. This put the blower on top of the funnel the wrong way round and caused a blowback, just as Bram decided to have a blow through the damper in order to clear the soot. It all came back in his face.

Just to make matters worse, the shrimp cooling net, which had not been lashed down, leapt skywards, spreading cooked shrimps everywhere. The copper boiled over, and brother Bram, snatching off the wooden lid, slammed it down on the deck - it promptly broke into several pieces. Laurie screamed with laughter at the spectacle. He was unable to contain himself. Brother Bram was not amused and promptly cuffed him round the ear, and a cuff from brother Bram was like being hit by a sledge-hammer, Laurie was tempted to hit back, but very wisely changed his mind.

The mixed fishing continued on through that summer, continuing to use a conventional shrimp beam trawl. Other types of trawls were being designed, but these included a much larger sized mesh. Father's insistence that whatever else happened, shrimps would always be their bread and butter, prevented any immediate change in policy, where the brothers were concerned, this attitude was also supported by Henry, but it was inevitable that changes would eventually come about.

Ray had already hand braided a net himself, called an otter trawl. He was anxious to give it a try, but this involved using diverters, instead of a beam to open the mouth of the trawl. All of these new additions to the fishery cost money, and lack of it meant that everything had to be done on the cheap.

Progress was slow but bound to come eventually, Ray had already ordered the wood to make the diverters. These were later to become recognized as otter boards, and became a basic part of fishing gear to be used for many years in the future.

Laurie was always keen on these experiments, he loved to play around with the trawls, making little changes which might improve the catching power of *Reindeer* and *Lady D*, but these changes always had to meet with the approval of Father or Ray. As Ray and Laurie were usually of one mind, he was allowed to learn his trade in the best possible way, by practical trial and error.

CHAPTER FORTY EIGHT

Laurie's personal and social life (when he was ashore) continued to develop in a satisfactory way. His love of gymnastics and sport of any kind never diminished in any way, and although scouting held no great appeal for him, he made many more friends because he was involved.

The relationship with Tina was a nice sort of bonus, but never took precedence over work, or sport.

During the summer months, while the weather was warm, he enjoyed riding his bike over to her village, and because of their friendship, received invitations to parties and special events. One party in particular which took place in the village, was really quite extraordinary. It started at three o'clock one Saturday afternoon and continued on until after midnight. Laurie went to the party with five other boys from his home town, travelling on the bus.

Although nothing really serious happened, it did turn into a bit of a riot.

Some thirty youngsters of both sexes were involved, they were having such a good time, that Laurie and his friends missed the last bus home.

The party would probably have continued all night, had it not been for the fact that several of the parents came looking for their sons and daughters in the early hours of the Sunday morning, which was probably just as well.

CHAPTER FORTY NINE

Even before Laurie rolled out of bed, he could hear the fog horn wailing.

Looking out of his bedroom window, he realized that visibility was down to about thirty yards - it was a typical late autumn morning.

There had been a slight frost, which meant that it was going to be cold until the sun rose high enough to clear the fog away.

Usually on a day such as this, the sky above would be cloudless, and eventually as the sun gained strength, become a beautiful day.

Thirty minutes later, he was pushing the old sack truck round onto the quay. It rattled considerably and was very noisy, but it served a useful purpose in as much as it carried the fuel containers to and from the quay. They did have another, much larger barrow, which had been named *Yock's Pride*. Father had built this himself, but it was only used to carry the catch or nets, obviously fuel and fish had to be kept well apart.

There was about a dozen fishermen gathered in the shelter which had always served as a meeting place. They were debating how long it would be before the fog cleared. Father was in favour of waiting a while, but Ray and Laurie wanted to get going. They had been doing quite well on the fish, but those days were now numbered as winter approached. A day lost, was a day that could never be regained. Once the older fishermen gathered and started talking, more fish were caught in the shelter than anywhere else.

This being the case, Ray and Laurie carried on to where

they loaded everything into the boat ready for sea. Father reluctantly followed. It was his opinion that the fog would clear, but become dense again once the sun had gone down.

When they let go of the moorings, it was still quite thick. Laurie was stationed as lookout on the forepeak, but he was not there for long, very soon the sun broke through and took control. By this time *Reindeer* was well on her way towards the wrecks where they intended to start fishing. It was their intention to work eastward on the ebb tide, and more than likely finish up well out to sea. With a full six hours of ebb tide in their favour, it was possible to tow the trawl many miles.

Laurie had been standing with his hand resting on the forestay, but the fog was lifting so fast, his presence there was no longer necessary. Before leaving his position, he took one last long look around, just to see if there were many ships under way. It was then that his eyes rested on one that would never move again, and become the talking point in committee rooms for decades.

She was an American liberty ship, full of high explosives. Through sheer negligence on the part of somebody, the ship had dropped anchor in such a position that when the tide started to turn and ebb she sat on top of a sandbank! Breaking her back and leaving her in two pieces. Because of her lethal cargo and close proximity to the land, no one person was prepared to take responsibility in attempting to move her, so she stayed a menace to all and a constant reminder of war. Laurie himself had good cause to remember this.

One day, just about a year ago while shrimping in the small open boat, he and Ray had been working quite close to the sunken ship, when fog closed in. They had just hauled the net and were busy stowing away in preparation to go home. It was almost low water, and as tide was very slack, they had not expected to move very much. Once again, Laurie was taught the lesson, never take the sea for granted.

That particular afternoon, the ebb tide kept running hard,

much later than usual. The first warning of danger, was when they bumped alongside the sunken ship's mast.

Thoughts of the eerie stillness as they lay amongst the remains of that torn ship, would remain alive in Laurie's memory for ever. When dense fog descended, he would always remember how the little boat had brushed against spars and rigging of the wreck and the thousands of tons of potential death which lay just underneath them. The engine had not been used to get clear, oars were shipped and they carefully threaded their way out of the carnage of what was once a beautiful ship, Expecting any minute to hear a tearing sound underneath, which would mean that a piece of unseen wreckage had ripped the boat's hull apart. They had been fortunate, what might have been a complete disaster, passed away as just another one of those unexpected happenings which take place almost every day in the life of men who go to sea.

Laurie could not stand dreaming about the past for ever, another half an hour and they would begin the day's fishing, This was far more important than anything that had happened in the past.

The sun now shone bright and clear, it was once again a lovely day, The net was soon streamed astern and everything being clear, lowered to the sea-bed. The fishing had begun. Fish swim neither on or off the sea-bed at all times. All species, under extreme circumstances, leave the bottom at some time, even if it be only a few feet or inches, Upheaval caused by tide or wind can lift even the strongest ground loving fish many fathoms from the depths of the sea. Darkness can also have the same effect, Laurie was to learn most of these things as time went on.

Each haul usually lasted about an hour. This depended mainly on the condition of each individual piece of ground being worked, and also the time of year. As winter approached, the weed and muck which often caused so much extra work, would die, then rot and disappear.

After the first haul, Laurie knew that cleaning the fish and shrimps today was not going to be a problem. It was not a big catch, but about right for the time of tide and the ground they had towed over. The catch should improve as they moved further out into deeper water, where it was hoped the fish would gather to feed at low water.

Laurie had just finished cleaning up after the first haul, and it had yielded one five gallon basket of shrimps, fifteen skate, a few soles and plaice, but also three sizable cod. This was a sure sign of winter coming on.

It was now almost mid-day, the sun had taken control of the weather, turning the murky haze into golden warmth. The copper fire crackled merrily and directly she boiled, Laurie would begin cooking the shrimps. There was always something to keep him busy.

The day progressed nicely, each haul a little better than the one before, and as the cool net began to fill up with golden brown shrimps, so the boxes of other fish increased accordingly. The low water haul was yet to come, with any luck it was going to be a bumper day. Father was not his usual contented self. As the afternoon wore on and the sun began to lose its power, so he became more restless. It was quite obvious that he was worried about the fog closing in at dusk, when the temperature dropped.

This was the last haul of the day, very shortly they would slow the engine down to its minimum speed and start to pull in on the warp, rope bridle, then would come the bridle block and the engine put into neutral. The *Reindeer* would swing round side on to what was left of the tide, and the usual race between Ray and Laurie, to get their end of the net up first, was on, but once again, by just a few inches, Laurie came second.

The last haul is not always best, but it was today, rounding off a really good day's fishing, but even as the large bag of fish swung aboard, the sun sunk out of sight, almost as if it was trying to escape from the dense fog which now closed in.

Normally, *Reindeer* would have been underway and steaming for home, within minutes of the cod end coming aboard, but under these conditions, this was out of the question. Father had always instilled in his sons that the first priority must always be to get the small unwanted fish back overboard, in order that they might have a chance to survive. He was a very caring man, and always looking towards the future.

Even now, under these difficult circumstances, not being able to see from stem to stern, he insisted on quickly sorting through the last haul before getting underway.

Laurie had no doubts in his mind where he would be spending the next three or four hours. Once the fish had been roughly separated and Father was ready to move, Laurie was ordered up to the forestay as look-out. He had proved more than once his ability to pick out objects which were invisible to other people. He was blessed with extremely sharp eyesight, but even so, with almost nil visibility, he doubted that it was going to make that much difference. If something happened to be dead ahead, the chances of steering clear in time to avoid a collision, were heavily loaded against them. But it was not all doom and gloom, Laurie knew exactly which course Father would take under these conditions, and was considering the obstacles which lay in their path.

As he stared into the blackness ahead, he pictured three sets of gun turrets. They had been erected for the specific purpose of stopping enemy bomber aircraft from taking a direct flight path to London. They were known as the forts or towers, and even now, although the war was over, they were manned by soldiers. It was not unusual for the boats to go alongside and give the troops a feed of fish, but in these conditions they became dangerous obstacles, and needed to be given a clear berth. Laurie guessed rightly that Father would keep to the south side of these, it would keep them out of the main channel, which they would cross later, as they came closer to home.

They had already passed one set of towers, Laurie estimated that the distance away was about three or four hundred yards, but it was very hard to judge. All three sets of towers were fitted with the same type of horn, but sounded at different intervals.

As the towers stood several miles apart, there was no chance of confusing one set with another. Laurie could now hear the distant whine of the second set above the sound of the *Reindeer's* engine. The fog was so thick that he could not even see his Father at the tiller, or Ray, who would be close to the engine hatch, ready to reach for the controls, and when necessary, swing the lead line.

Their course was going to take them very close to the second set of towers, but Laurie hoped not close enough to be dangerous. The legs on which they stood were made of solid reinforced concrete, with bits and pieces sticking out everywhere, they would make short work of *Reindeer* if she were to collide with one of them.

The whine of the horn grew louder, Laurie shouted a warning that although it was to starboard, the sound seemed terribly close.

In his imagination, Laurie saw the legs of those towers a dozen times in the next two minutes, but he knew that if he did see them, they would be real, very real.

Father altered course five degrees to port, and this alone saved a very nasty accident, probably even their lives.

The horn sounded again, it was so loud, Laurie thought he must be right underneath it, and that's precisely where he was. It sounded again, at the same moment as he saw the tower leg, no more than ten feet away.

His warning shout would have been of little use, had they been on the wrong side of the leg, because it would have meant that they were in the middle of the mighty concrete towers, without a dog's chance of survival. Laurie heaved a great sigh of relief as he realized how close they had come to disaster.

There were many varied reasons why that particular day was deeply imprinted on Laurie's mind, not the least of these being that it was the fifth of November, yes, Guy Fawkes night, and Laurie had promised to go out with his friends over to Tina's village, where there was to be a big bonfire and plenty of fireworks. But for *Reindeer*, the long, painfully slow journey home continued and seemed to go on forever. Sitting on the stemhead or leaning against the forestay, Laurie's vigil lasted almost four hours.

He was soaked through to the skin, in spite of his two jumpers and top coat. The freezing cold fog had penetrated into his bones, but he stayed alert, his eyes never ceasing to try to pierce the terrible blackness ahead. It occurred to Laurie that at times it was as if he had lost all sense of reality, Everything in the world had ceased to exist apart from the throb of *Reindeer's* diesel engine, and the void ahead which held everything and yet remained empty. He felt ready to deal with any eventuality which might occur, and yet at the same time his limbs were numb and incapable of movement.

Laurie shook himself and buffed his arms vigorously. Had he heard something, or was it his imagination once again playing tricks?

The sound came again, no mistake this time, it was definitely a bucket being rattled. Someone along-side the Pier could hear the sound of *Reindeer's* engine and was banging the bucket with a piece of metal, in order to guide them safely alongside.

Reindeer was barely moving now. She had to come in very slowly. Visibility could not be more than a few feet and the boat actually bumped against the wall before Laurie was aware that the slight change of colour in the fog above his head, was the Pier light. They were home.

It must have been almost ten o'clock that night when at last they left the boat, but it made not the slightest difference to Laurie. He was indoors, washed, changed, and away out, inside of thirty minutes.

His friends were waiting for him, and in spite of the fog managed to find their way to the bonfire. It never entered his head that he might have to do the same thing all over again tomorrow - it was enough to live for tonight.

CHAPTER FIFTY

On looking back over the adventures of his life and all those escapades he became involved in, Laurie came to the conclusion that in every true fisherman, there has to be a little bit of madness.

Putting out to sea in search of fish, is not just another job, it is a way of life.

As events turned out the next day, Laurie did not have to concern himself about another day in the fog. It remained too dense to go out for almost three days.

The work carried on just the same. Even when conditions made it impossible for Laurie and his brothers to fish, there was always plenty of refitting or repairing of gear to be carried out ashore.

It was strange how the neighbours accepted all the disturbances they had to put up with because fishermen lived in their road.

There were four fishing families in the little cul-de-sac where Laurie lived, Myrtle Road, and another seven in the larger road which ran across the top Hartington Road and led straight down to the sea front. Every fisherman had his own barrow or sack truck, which would rattle and bang down the road at all times of the night, but there were never any complaints, in spite of the noise it created, with all the comings and goings. Laurie could remember back to the days when he was at school, and his father went out in the night. It was possible to hear the sound of wheels on paving stones from house to sea front, and he would lay in bed listening and wondering how many people had been awakened by the clatter.

One of the many jobs which became part of routine work, was tying little corks on the underside of shrimp nets. It was supposed to be a remedy to stop chaffing on the sea bed, but Laurie never felt that it was very successful. The brothers would spend a whole day sitting in the road, the net pulled from one side to the other, sowing on these silly corks, only to see them all torn off in a minute, if something heavy was caught in the net while fishing. Laurie was convinced that there must be a better way, and in later years, all these old fashioned methods changed drastically, but for the moment this was the way things had to be done.

It did not occur to Laurie at the time, that although there were plenty of cars and vans about, not one of the fishermen possessed a motor vehicle. So far as he could remember, Father was one of the first .

Each day when they landed, the shrimps, which were carried in large sacks, had to be tipped out into a long tin bath and measured into five gallon stockings. They were then tied and labelled, ready for market.

The next part of the operation was no mean task, and it usually fell on Laurie's shoulders to carry it out.

The shrimps for market were always despatched from Central Station. It was up hill all the way, and a steep climb at that. Laurie would push up to twenty of these five gallon stockings, to the station at any one time.

Yock's Pride, the special barrow which Father had built himself, was kept for this job, but it was very big and clumsy for one person to handle or control. Laurie much preferred putting wooden fish box lids on the old sack truck, and piling the sacks as high as possible, sometimes so high, he could not see over the top, and where he was heading.

Laurie had a choice of three different ways to the station, first was what he called the short sharp death. This was obviously a very steep hill and a tremendous challenge when carrying twenty bags of shrimps, but it was the shortest and most direct route. The other two were a more steady climb, but took longer, and it was push hard all the way. Laurie usually chose the short sharp death.

On one occasion, Laurie had decided that with a full load, he would take the short route. He knew that he was capable even if it was tough going. Having taken a rest, he put all his weight on the handles and pushed, the first part was the worst. Head down and straining hard, he appeared to be moving nicely on up the hill, but gradually the load seemed to get heavier. He strained even harder, but came to a dead stop. He had no idea why, but he was not going to make it.

Full of frustration, Laurie was on the point of turning round and going the other way, when he heard laughter, (remember he could not see over the top), on looking round the side, and preparing to do battle, he was greatly relieved to see two of his mates leaning on the sack truck, laughing their heads off. No wonder it had been so hard.

They were soon on the other side, pushing with him, and all was well, but that was the hardest push Laurie could remember, and would always remember in the days ahead.

Those three days of fog were by far the worst and long lasting that Laurie was to experience throughout his fishing life. At the end of the third day, it turned into rain and once more the boats put to sea.

CHAPTER FIFTY ONE

Henry and Bram did not enjoy a very good relationship. They caught the shrimps all right, but were never really comfortable with each other. This was not a very satisfactory state of affairs, when one considers the many hours spent alone together in a small boat. Father decided that maybe it was time for changes to be made, and as a result of this, Laurie found himself aboard the *Lady D*, working with Henry, for the duration of the winter.

He was not unduly bothered which of the two boats he worked on in winter, as both would be fishing for shrimps. He enjoyed the work and general routine of picking out the rubbish and sifting the shrimps before they were cooked. There were at that time some thirty shrimp boats working the area. Considering how little demand and limited outlets there was, it was far too many. Laurie could not imagine in the near future, anything which was going to change this situation, but for some time he would have very little say in the matter.

On his first trip with Henry aboard *Lady D* it poured cats and dogs all day, not the best of weather for catching and cooking shrimps, but they got along fine.

It soon became obvious to Laurie why Bram could not get along with Henry. He had some most annoying habits. There might be a whole deck full of shrimps, waiting to go through the processing routine, but if he saw one big shrimp which was about to go through the scuppers overboard - that one shrimp became of paramount importance, taking precedence over all else.

Laurie found this most amusing, and when Henry was not looking, he would go round the deck, placing shrimps about two inches from the scupper holes, just for the pleasure of seeing Henry rushing to pick them up.

Henry also had a habit of trying to carry out all of his tasks standing down in the engine room hatch. This was just not feasible, and one time at least proved very painful, and it happened to be on Laurie's first day aboard *Lady D*.

They were about halfway through the day. Henry was standing in his usual position in the hatchway, his feet on the engine room floorboards. Incidently, Henry took great care of his money, and had just purchased himself a new oilskin, of which he was very proud, this was it's first day in use. It was absolutely pelting down with rain, but with his sou'wester on to stop water going down inside his oilskin, Henry was quite happy. What Henry did not realize was that his lovely new waxed calico oilskin had spread out down below like a ballroom gown, and each time he turned round in the hatch, was within a fraction of an inch of the rear end spark plug of the engine. It was inevitable, that eventually, with the water cascading down his oilskin, the two were going to make contact. And they did. As the charge of electricity went through him, Henry shot his arms skywards with a scream of surrender. The engine stopped, and Laurie stood laughing in disbelief.

Laurie was fast approaching his sixteenth birthday. Life was good, and he had no complaints to speak of. Money was never very plentiful, but this was nothing new. His first week's money on leaving school, had been ten shillings, of which he gave his mother half, at Father's suggestion. His best week had been the fantastic sum of five pounds, of which he also gave his mother half, but he only received that huge amount once. Father assured him that on his sixteenth birthday, he would be on half share. Laurie could never quite work out if this was good or bad, because sometimes there was nothing to share out. But money did not rate very high in his interests.

Fishing, football, gymnastics and girl friends, that was the order of his priorities, with a couple of good films thrown in each week, if there was time. His Sundays always belonged to the church, Father said so, and Laurie agreed.

It was still several days to go until Laurie's birthday.

The boats were both fishing the same grounds, the shrimps were plentiful and so far had they had managed to keep this information from anyone else. It was most important when shrimps were in short supply, that if a new piece of ground was found, and the catch was good, it must be kept secret at all costs.

They had been on the grounds two days, and this would be the third. The combined catches of both boats amounted to more than a hundred gallons each day.

There was one little problem however, the catch was a mixture of pink and brown shrimps. They were good quality, but as yet Father had not been informed from the market, what sort of price they were making.

Father was of the opinion that shrimps being so scarce, the price should be good, but they would not find out until they landed that day.

Father was in for a disappointment. On reaching home, he was told that the shrimps had made two shillings a gallon; about half the price he had expected, but they would have been worth four shillings, had they not been mixed. He was more than put out with this news, but there was nothing he could do, well, that's how it looked at first, but as Father always said, 'Where there's a will, there's a way.'

The living room table was cleared to receive the catch, and all available hands sat round the table, separating pink from brown. Laurie wondered, as he sat at the table, with his fingers picking at top speed, 'Was it always so difficult, earning a living, or did Father just choose the hardest ways?'

As Laurie had seen many times before, Father refused to be beaten, even if the odds were stacked high against him. He may have had his faults, he might never become rich, but whatever the out-come, he was one hell of a man.

Lauries sixteenth birthday heralded a fresh start in many ways. First of all the news arrived that Peter was coming home and wished to get back into fishing. Laurie was quite happy about this. The two of them had enjoyed much fun together, surviving many scrapes, especially when they were on the canal barges.

Second, came the rather surprising announcement that Ray intended to take advantage of a Government scheme, designed to help young fishermen with the building of new boats. This brought great excitement and Laurie got the feeling that progress was being made at last. It was certainly not before time.

The old boats were continually having their seams corked with oakem, but more than once had come close to disaster. They were old, and just not up to the rough kind of punishment they were taking.

Lady D with Henry and Laurie on board, had one very nasty experience, and was almost lost. They had put to sea one morning with a fresh, but not strong, south westerly wind.

The sky had a menacing look about it, but as they intended working in comparatively sheltered waters, they were not unduly concerned. The grounds for which they were heading, lay some twenty two miles south, south east from Southend. This would bring them under the shelter of the coast of Kent. It was a considerable distance away from home, for the *Lady D*, but they had been taking a lot more risks lately, in their efforts to earn more money.

At first all went well, they arrived on the grounds without mishap, and as expected, the conditions were ideal, just a little ground swell to keep the water a good colour, but no sign of any broken white caps to make it uncomfortable.

Fishing had gone well, the cool net was still full and already Laurie was filling the fourth sack with big golden brown shrimps. They were now on their last haul, and with a little bit of luck, would soon be on the way home.

Laurie happened to glance out over the port side towards the land, at the same time putting more shrimps from the boiler onto the cool net. A fresh breeze brought steam from the hot shrimps back into his face. He loved that smell, it always gave him an irresistible urge to eat some, and he most probably would have, if something else had not caught his eye. Well to the west of them, and only just visible on the horizon, was a long black line of impenetrable cloud. From that moment on, everything went into top gear. Hauling the net and getting lashed and battened down took about fifteen minutes, even so, the depression was moving so fast from the west, that a shadow lay above them, momentarily the wind had dropped.

As Henry put the engine full ahead, the same thought was in both of their minds, and the thought turned to reality in the next few minutes, the wind flew north west and came like a shot out of a gun, from nothing, to full gale force in seconds, and the *Lady D* was completely exposed to a blast of wind, such as she had never encountered before.

Lady D had not been built to withstand the terrible battering that was being forced upon her, she was making water badly, through several seams, and there was absolutely nothing her crew could do about it. Laurie manned the main bilge pump for the whole of the four and a half hour steam home. Henry stood at the helm, dressed in his oilskin and sou'wester, but blinded with spray. The decks were awash from stem to stern.

Although it was still daylight, it might just as well have been night, for all the difference it made. Every now and again, when he could clear his eyes, Henry would quickly slide open the engine room hatch, have a look down below, then close it again. The water was almost up to the floorboards, they were fighting a losing battle.

Grabbing the dip bucket, Henry kept the rope which was always attached to it, in his hand. Then each time he opened the hatch, down would go the bucket, coming back up full of water. He repeated this several times, before closing the hatch. Just the fact that it was possible for him to do this, meant that the prop shaft was now well under water - the situation was desperate.

The *Lady D* had now been steaming almost four hours and had managed to reach the north side of the main shipping channel, but it was doubtful that she would get much further. There was so much water in the well of the stricken little boat, that Henry expected the engine to stop any minute. Once that happened, she would swing round side to the swell, and be swamped.

Laurie was still pumping, he had hardly spoken to his brother throughout the long steam for home, there was not much point, they both knew what would happen if he ceased pumping. Laurie had not given it a thought before, but suddenly it occurred to him that neither of them could swim. It was about the only sport in which he had never taken any interest, and now it appeared it might have been the most important.

Lady D, with her flat bottom, had crashed into the swell so many times, with bone jarring regularity, that Laurie's teeth ached, his muscles were void of all feeling.

He wanted to stop pumping, but his movements were now automatic, it was just like being in a dream.

Such was his state of mind, he thought his imagination was playing tricks on him. The vicious swell appeared to have died away, but he could think of no reason why it should, he kept pumping, but he was aware that Henry had passed him in the dark, walking forward. It was now night, the wind still screamed, but they were laying in calm water, he must be dreaming.

The giant tanker lay half into the wind, and half across the tide. At anchor, she was creating a false harbour, but false or otherwise, she was the saviour of the *Lady D*, now laying quietly under her protective bulk.

Now that her seams had stopped working, she was taking in much less water, and the two brothers were able to get her almost dry, before making the last short dash for home, but it had been a close call.

After the terrible punishment she received on that fateful day, *Lady D* was never quite the same again.

Arrangements were made for slipping and re-fastening her planking the following day, but it was obvious the brave little boat had sustained damages that just could not be repaired sufficiently to put her back into full time service.

Nevertheless, as nothing else was available for the moment, Father decided that she would have to be used until another boat could be found.

CHAPTER FIFTY TWO

Brother Peter's arrival back on the scene, only added to Father's problems. Somehow another boat had to be found. There was some talk of using *The Boys* again for catching shrimps, but Father was against this, winter was almost on them and he had no intention of letting any of his sons spend another full winter in an open boat. There had to be another way, but fortunately the matter resolved itself.

Operating in Laurie's home town was a company who owned several passenger boats and they were quite a thriving concern. At the height of the previous summer season, one of their skippers had spoken to Father about the possibility of Laurie going to work for them. They needed a hand who was capable of handling a small boat. Laurie's antics in rowing and sculling with one oar on the stern had become well known.

Father had talked to him about it, but as expected, Laurie refused. It was his one aim in life to be a fisherman, not a boatman. He had turned the offer down flat.

Since that time, the same company had purchased one of the old type Bawley boats and installed a new engine. She was a very heavily built vessel with large oak frames and in excellent condition. The installation of a thirty horsepower Lister diesel, had transformed her into a very formidable little ship.

The Valory had been fishing for several months without much success, when Peter arrived home. It appeared that the company had employed more than one skipper and different crews, but they were losing money and growing rather desperate about the situation.

Once more they approached Father with another proposition. Would he be interested in chartering the *The Valory* on a share basis, giving him full control of the vessel.

Father considered this a gift from heaven. She was a fine ship, and certainly with the progress his sons were making, would be a great asset to his plans.

So it was all arranged. Henry, Peter and Laurie took over the *The Valory*. At last they had a powerful boat, with tremendous potential. This, combined with the fact that Ray was going ahead with his own boat, and the keel was soon to be laid, gave Laurie a great feeling of enthusiasm. The family was moving ahead now at some considerable speed, and it was at this time that the decision was taken to purchase the old green Ford van, a box wagon which was to be the instrument of so many adventures.

CHAPTER FIFTY THREE

There had been a quick change in Laurie's social life, and all because of a bet with one of his friends. His visits to see Tina had become less frequent. This was not something which had been planned, it just worked out that way. Arriving home from sea after a long hard day, made it difficult to keep a regular relationship going. It made matters worse when Tina changed schools. She was no longer just around the corner most of the day, as she had been before. Gradually they had grown apart, but their friendship, although not serious, remained intact for many years.

Laurie had kept contact with the Scouts and continued teaching gymnastics every troupe night. A strong bond of fellowship had grown out of that first unusual arrangement which had been made to get the Scouts started. Harry was now an established Scoutmaster, but he was extremely pleased and surprised that he had managed to keep the boys together. The pact to share the hall had been a great success, some of the lads even attended church with Laurie on Sunday. It caused a bit of a rumpus when they arrived, usually ten minutes late. There was a good reason for this, Laurie had to leave home at least an hour before services commenced - it took him that time to round them all up.

Colin and Peter Kidwell were perhaps Laurie's closest friends, They were never far apart and although Colin was a year younger, They had spent much time at each other's homes, he and Peter had also been to sea with Laurie on several occasions in the summer.

They both had tremendous wit and were always setting people up and that also included Laurie. They had dashed into church one Sunday morning, late as always, and sat down at the back. This placed them directly in line with an attractive young lady, who sat at a table, keeping the attendance records. Laurie had known her family for a long time, but she mixed with a much older crowd and he had always considered her a little bit out of his class. Looking across at her, it was impossible not to notice her long slender legs, stretched out underneath the table. Just at that precise moment, Laurie's mind was anywhere, but in church.

Colin, always quick off the mark, picked up the line of Laurie's interest. Giving him a dig in the ribs, he whispered, "Ten bob, if you can get a date." Laurie hesitated, quite sure he was about to lose ten shillings, but in spite of this, he could not resist the challenge. Without realizing the significance of that one word, he said "Done." Having accepted the bet, Laurie could not help but keep glancing across at the young woman he was about to ask out for an evening. She appeared to be very mature, rather like Rita had been, in what now seemed like another life, so long ago. He began to feel a little bit nervous, and just to increase his sense of insecurity, the young woman, whose name was Doris, became aware that she was being stared at, and tucking her legs under the chair, on which she sat, cool, calm and collected, returned his gaze. Laurie wanted to look away, but another dig in the ribs from Colin, reminded him of the bet, so he took a chance and smiled at her. Much to his relief, she smiled back and Laurie could feel the blood racing through his veins.

Colin lost that bet. Four years later Doris became Laurie's wife.

CHAPTER FIFTY FOUR

Why it happened, Laurie was never quite able to comprehend, but there was no doubt whatsoever that it did. Whenever he and Peter came together, many strange, funny, and often ridiculous things seemed to happen.

No sooner had Peter arrived back home, than the combination sparked off one adventure after another, it was almost as if they looked for trouble, which was not really true, trouble just seemed to come their way.

In spite of the years that had passed since they were on the canal barges, it was as if they had never been separated, it was a simple case of taking up where they had left off.

Peter had only been home a few days when he bought his first motor bike. All his life, he loved big powerful cars and motor bikes. It was a craze which remained with him throughout the whole of his life. The old Ford box wagon had not yet come into commission, some repairs were being carried out to prepare it for the ordeals that it would have to endure in the future.

Reindeer and *The Valory* were now two quite formidable boats with considerable catching power. They needed to be if they were going to support the whole of the Gilson family.

The boats had landed a good catch of shrimps, well over two hundred gallons, forty three five gallon stockings which would have to be pushed up hill to the station. Father's big barrow, *Yock's Pride*, would have to be used, there were far too many for the old sack truck.

It had been a long and tiring day, the boats had been at sea more than twelve hours. Even with two baths and measures going at full speed, it would be at least another hour before they were ready for the push up the hill. As the two youngest, this duty would fall on Peter and Laurie. Not a task for the faint hearted. It was going to be hard going, but they had already anticipated and discussed the problem. They had a plan. At last, *Yock's Pride* was loaded and all ready to go. Father had checked the labels on each sack and stood back, removing his cap to scratch his head - an old familiar habit, when contemplating a problem. He doubted that the two boys could manage on their own. It was a hard push to the station with such a heavy load. The boys assured him that once they were up the first part and out of the cul-de-sac, they could manage. From there to the next hill, it was reasonably flat, about one hundred and fifty yards. So Father gave way, against his better judgment. They all pushed *Yock's Pride* up the first part and left Peter and Laurie to go the rest alone. It was easy going along the flat, *Yock's Pride* ran smoothly, but directly after they had turned the corner, the boys stopped. This was part of the prearranged plan. Peter dashed off down the road, Returning within five minutes on his motor bike, a piece of rope coiled on the handle bars.

In seconds, the rope was attached, and probably for the first time ever, the motor bike was towing a trailer, with Peter glancing nervously back over his shoulder, and Laurie trotting happily along behind, balancing and steering *Yock's Pride*. It worked like a dream, until they crossed the main high street, where a Police-man stood on duty, he was taken too much by surprise to make any attempt to stop them on the way up, but he was firmly blocking the road when they came back. With a group of laughing spectators standing around, who had witnessed the most unusual sight, the policeman protested that you could not tow a barrow with a motor cycle. The two brothers, in all innocence, stated that they just did, and although, up to that moment, his face had been very serious, it now spread into a wide grin. "Go on, you young beggars, clear off and don't try it again or I'll be down to have a word with your father." Peter and Laurie managed to keep a guilty look on their faces, until they were round the corner out of sight, then they laughed until they cried - the look on that copper's face had been a picture.

In exactly the same way as Laurie resumed his relationship with Peter, Henry and Peter also carried on feuding. They had some sort of friction between them which would burst into flame at the slightest provocation.

Laurie now found himself working aboard a boat where they all depended so much on each other, that really there was no room for discord. So often, one false move or a wrong decision could mean the loss of a limb or even life itself, but fortunately this never happened to any of the Gilson brothers. They suffered crushed fingers and mangled hands, dislocated joints and pulled muscles. The sea took its toll on each one of them. All of these injuries and discomforts, which they shrugged off and brushed aside, came back to plague them in later years, but looking back, Laurie realized that it was a miracle that not one of them were actually lost at sea through accident, but they had many close shaves.

One morning, they all turned out ready for sea. An argument started about the formation of unlit buoys along the northern side of the channel. This time, it was not a heated affair which turned to blows, but more a conflict of opinions which resulted in a ducking. What little wind there was, came from the south, but it only amounted to a light breeze, certainly nothing to prevent the boats from fishing that day. It was on the flood tide, and at the precise moment when they started the discussion, three hours before high water. If there was fuel, salt or any gear to be taken aboard *Reindeer* or *The Valory,* it was normal procedure to get the big skiff underway. If all the gear was aboard, then it was possible for them to go from the beach in the little boat which was kept chained up on the sea wall.

On this particular morning, there were two five gallon water bottles and one sack of salt. Laurie just assumed that they would need the big skiff and proceeded to unchain the little boat. He dragged her down to the beach and having shipped the oars, was about to push off , when a shout from the wall stopped him. "No need to bother with the skiff, Lol, we can manage in the punt this morning." Laurie was surprised, to say the least; at twelve stone, he was the smallest, his brothers ranged up to seventeen stone. Five of them, plus fifty six pounds of salt, plus two fresh water containers, making up another sixty pounds, it was expecting rather a lot of the little punt, after all she was only twelve feet long. His brothers walked down from the quay, they continued their argument even as they climbed into the punt. Having stowed both salt and water containers, they stepped aboard, two forward and two aft - Laurie sat on the middle thwart and rowed. Any other time Laurie would have mentioned that the punt had very little freeboard, but the argument was becoming more heated by the second, although about to be cooled considerably.

Dawn was breaking as they pulled away from the beach, turning the black of night into the cold grey of a winter's day. The slapping of wavelets coming over the stem, was drowned by a constant drone of voices still in dispute about the buoys. They had only moved some twenty yards, when Laurie made his first protest that she was shipping a drop of water. It met with very little response. His next protest was more urgent, but even as he spoke, the water was swilling round his ankles. The next ten minutes was pure comedy. The punt gurgled her objections, as she sunk underneath the five brothers. All thoughts about buoys were forgotten, as freezing cold water rose suddenly up over their private parts. Peter gasped as he sunk up to his chest, and then got the shock of his life, as Henry, shouting "I can't swim," clasped him to his bosom, both arms locked firmly round Peter, a sight Laurie had never seen before or ever expected to see again. But Peter's next remark completed the scene, "Get off, you silly sod, my feet are on the bottom," there was less than five feet of water.

CHAPTER FIFTY FIVE

Old Sam and Young Sam, were another typical combination of a long line of seagoing fishermen. Once again Young Sam, (now aged about fifty) was the last of his line, but would remain Young Sam until his father, Old Sam, (now nearly eighty) passed on, but of course, he was no longer involved in the fishing.

Young Sam had a very dry sense of humour. Laurie had never heard him raise his voice and in fact, never made conversation unless he had something interesting or important to say.

On the morning of the great swim, Sam had been standing on the jetty with the brothers and listening to their argument. He did not join in, but possibly raised a thankful prayer to Heaven for not giving him any brothers.

By his comments, it was obvious he derived great pleasure from the predicaments that the boys got themselves into, but he also had a great admiration for them because they would never give up as they refused to be beaten.

These sentiments and feelings were made known to Laurie many years later.

Young Sam now stood on the quay shaking his head in disbelief. He had watched as they pulled away from the beach, and thought at the time that once again they were pushing their luck. Even so, to look down and see the five brothers walking back, pulling the punt behind them, was even too much for him. He quoted

'Five valiant brothers put to sea in a boat.

Their brave little craft, looking good and afloat.
But something's amiss - did they make a wrong tack?
For here were the brothers all walking back.'

Young Sam's humour was lost on the boys at that moment, but as the years went by, Laurie was to tell the story on many occasions. It always made for a good laugh, even if some did think that he made them up as he went along.

The next morning, Young Sam and several other fishermen were having the usual chat under the shelter, before going to sea. The five brothers just stopped for a second and one of them said "He who hesitates is lost." Young Sam was ready with his reply "But the wages of sin is death, or a ducking."

Laurie had a lot of respect and liking for Young Sam. It may have been because of his humour or more likely the fact that he never appeared to be in a hurry. Some of the fishermen were inclined to be noisy and content to spend far too much time in the pubs, when they had the money, but not so with Sam, he took life at a steady pace, always giving the impression that whatever the circumstances, he would not be one to flap.

In many ways, Sam was the complete opposite to the Gilson brothers, so different in every way, but then he was twenty five years older, and had lived a whole lifetime at sea. Being the only son of a successful fisherman, he had inherited one of the best boats in the fleet, and an engine which seldom gave any trouble, his situation and opportunities were so far removed from the brothers, it would not be fair to make a comparison.

CHAPTER FIFTY SIX

That winter was not too severe. Most of the boats managed to survive and make a reasonable living, mostly from the shrimp fishing, but there were twelve of the bigger boats which would change gear and fish for sprats. Sam's boat was one of these.

Laurie loved to see the boats come home, deep loaded with the lovely silver fish, and if possible get down into the hold and help Sam unload.

Stowboating was a very old fashioned way of catching fish like sprats, herrings and pilchards, sometimes even a few cod. But the day was not far off when it was to be replaced by something far more efficient.

Laurie often listened to the old fishermen talk of the days when as many as a hundred stowboaters were at work, and would head straight up to London with their catch, but that was in the days of sail.

In the spring of that year, Laurie came to know Young Sam much better.

Sam's regular mate was taken ill, and Father was approached with a request for his youngest son's services. As things worked out, it only lasted two weeks, but it was long enough to show Laurie a completely different approach to fishing.

On the first morning, they turned out at high water. There was a fresh breeze from a south westerly direction. The chances were, it would fade away with the ebb tide, and Laurie's brothers put to sea, but not so Sam. Laurie was most surprised when he turned away saying "We'll give it best this morning, Lol, and turn out same time tomorrow, you can have the day off ."

This was unheard of for Laurie, a day off, when it was obvious that the wind was going to drop. That was his first lesson in difference of approach, and there was much more to come.

The following morning was clear and fine. Being first on the quay, Laurie had Sam's skiff alongside, ready and waiting, tholes shipped and oars at the ready. Sam climbed aboard and took one oar, Laurie said nothing, in spite of the fact that he longed to get hold of that other oar. As they pulled away from the jetty, Laurie put his weight on the oar as usual, with the intention of making the beautifully shaped skiff surge through the water. "Steady lad" said Sam, "you don't want to break the oar, there will be another day tomorrow."

Laurie eased back on the power and let Sam set the pace, he had entered another dimension, perhaps it would be best just to do as he was told, to begin with, and see how things worked out. Compared with what he was used to, it was like slow motion, methodical and thorough, but very slow.

Laurie was to learn many lessons in those two weeks with Sam and also suffer much frustration, but once again it was all good experience.

Sam was a man with a lifelong routine of never doing things in a hurry. It was not his policy to force the pace or take chances, he had no need. It had never once in his life been a case of fighting for existence, and it showed in his approach.

Sam was an extremely good fisherman, steady and sure of himself. He never went for the extra shilling if it involved taking a risk. These were things that Laurie could understand and take in for future reference, even if it was against his nature.

At the beginning of their two weeks together. Sam insisted on doing everything.

It would be a case of "Hold the helm, Lol, and I'll make

a cup of tea," or "I'll see to picking out and cooking the shrimps."

Thinking about it later, Laurie came to the conclusion that perhaps Sam wanted to make the work easier for him, and not put him under any pressure, but at that point in time, Laurie had only one thought, and that was to get involved in the real work, he hated standing around watching other people do things in which he excelled. But it had to happen gradually, and it took about three days for him to get Sam around to his way of thinking. Fortune also played its part.

It was the third day that they had fished together, and were hauling for the first time that day. They had almost got the trawl aboard, when Sam slightly pulled a muscle in his back. He insisted that he was alright, but was obviously in some pain, and had it been the beginning of the week, would certainly have stopped fishing and headed for home, but there were customers to be supplied and they needed the shrimps. Even so, he was considering letting go the anchor for an hour in order to get the first haul clear.

It took a while, but Laurie managed to convince him that they could manage, so long as the pain was not too much.

By the time the day came to an end, Sam had no doubts in his mind that Laurie was quite capable of taking care of things. The position had been reversed, and it was Laurie nursing Sam along and doing most of the work, and it continued that way for the rest of the two weeks. They became very good friends.

When Sam's regular mate returned, Laurie was assured that if ever he needed a berth, there would always be one for him aboard the *Souvenir.* Laurie was pleased to hear this, but thought he would be looking for a far more exciting life than he was likely to find with Young Sam. As it was, he received two very good weeks wages, which incidently, all went into the coffers, to be shared out with the family.

CHAPTER FIFTY SEVEN

So many things happened in the spring and summer, when Laurie began courting Doris, it would be impossible to relate everything that took place.

The importance of that time was perhaps lost in the sheer excitement, adventure and joy of being alive.

When Laurie approached the table where Doris sat, he was very nervous.

He had hardly spoken to the girl before this time, and as with Rita, he had that feeling of inferiority, but he had not the slightest idea why.

Laurie made conversation at first by making an apology for the fact that they caused a disturbance coming in late. He went on to explain that his friends did not normally attend church and that it took time to round them all up and bring them in. His conversation seemed to run out and quietly he said "Would you consider coming with me to see a film?" To his complete amazement, she accepted, he had not only got a date beyond his dreams, he had also won ten shillings, which was not bad going for one Sunday morning.

As arranged, he arrived outside the cinema, It would have been no surprise if she had not turned up, but there she stood waiting for him, and the very fact that she was early made his heart race. He wanted this evening to be a success more than anything in his life before, and it was, beyond all his expectations. Their friendship developed slowly but passionately, into a deep, thrilling love, a love beyond anything he could have imagined at that time.

Meanwhile, the old green Ford van had come into commission. There was one rather serious problem, however. Only Father had a driving licence, but this was not something that was going to stand in the way of progress, and all of the brothers, apart from Henry, took turns to drive the van, much against Father's wishes, who, although still very much respected, was beginning to lose control of his five sons. On the fishing side, as in most things, the changes took place at an alarming speed.

The war was now something that just happened, progress was the all important thing.

The boat that Ray was having built, was well on the way. Once the keel had been laid, the vessel appeared to grow every day.

Whenever Laurie and Doris could manage it, they would take a twenty six mile bus ride to inspect the progress. It was also a good excuse for them to get out and be alone together, they were magic moments. Sometimes it frightened Laurie a little that the depth of their emotions would overcome self control. They wanted each other permanently, but as yet were only half way through their seventeenth year. Doris was six weeks older than Laurie, but even so would not become seventeen for another five months.

Laurie had been accepted into Doris's home, after token resistance from her parents.

He was now firmly established and could do no wrong as far as the mother was concerned, but any talk of an engagement would be out of the question with both sets of parents, they were considered far too young. It was indeed fortunate that Laurie did have a very full life.

Each day now, the boats were becoming more venturesome, pushing further and further out to sea. The nets increased in size and designs altered constantly. Both *Reindeer* and *The Valory* now carried otter trawls, similar to the one which Ray had made some time before, but there was still a reluctance on the part of many fishermen to use them, purely because it resulted in more fish, but less shrimps.

In spite of the increased power, size of boats and dimensions of nets being used, not one of the vessels being operated at that time possessed a powered capstan or winch. It was not surprising that the fishermen of those days developed big muscles and enormous hands. Their bodies were under pressure for most of the time spent at sea.

The Valory powered through the water at about nine knots, she was bound for an area which the brothers had not previously worked, it was some twenty five miles from home, but as it was now the middle of summer and the weather fine, Laurie was looking forward to an interesting day.

They were going in search of pink shrimps. Before the war these grounds had been quite famous for the large juicy pink shrimps which came there in the warm water to feed and spawn on the Ross banks. These banks were riddled with tiny worms, the shrimps loved them and came in their millions to enjoy the dainty morsels. It was an old fishing prediction that if you found the Ross, you would find the shrimps.

When *The Valory* arrived at the west end of a six mile stretch of ground recognized as a starting point, several boats from different ports were already at work. Visibility was good, and so far as Laurie could tell, by the amount of the action aboard each boat, no one had yet made a haul.

Smoke poured from boiler funnels, showing that they had all got great expectations. It was unusual to light the copper fires until the first haul was aboard, but Laurie could see that every boat was working the little try-net similar to the one which had been used for the weed, when they had been peternet fishing, only much heavier.

They always carried a try net with them and no sooner had the gear been streamed and sunk away to the bottom, the try net quickly followed, and Laurie lit the copper fire all was ready.

Although they were fishing in seven fathoms of water , it was often possible to see the ripples made by the Ross banks.

Each time Henry had a look in the try net, it gave an indication of changes in character of the ground that was being fished.

After towing for thirty five minutes, the try net had yielded very little, just old oyster shells, one or two whelks and just the odd pink shrimp, but some of the boats ahead of them had started to haul.

Laurie walked along the deck just as Henry pulled up the try net once more. He could tell even before it was clear of the water, that it held more of something than at any other time that day.

Excitedly, Henry shot the contents out on the stern. There were several lumps of the Ross, almost the size of a man's fist, absolutely filled with tiny worms, but much more important a double handful of big bouncing pink shrimps. It was indeed time to haul.

Fifty fathoms of warp had to be pulled in before they reached the double block and bridles All three brothers stood in line and pulled with a rhythmic movement, which continued without a break until the block came up over the stern. Peter took one bridle, Laurie the other. Henry put the engine in neutral at the same time, pushing the helm hard over, so that *The Valory* came side to tide - incidentally the tide was running very hard. Gradually, as the two brothers pulled, boat and gear came together, the beam came to the surface almost dead level, which was as it should be, this kept equal weight between the two.

Apart from watching closely, in case anything should go wrong, there was only one thought at the back of Laurie's mind, 'what would be in the cod end?'

As they pulled the ground rope aboard and started putting weight on each selvedge

Peter and Laurie looked at each other with a knowing look and smiled, the cod end was heavy, but it was movable, not dead weight - things looked promising.

As they put the hoisting strop on, Laurie could see the noses of several skate sticking, out of the shrimps. It was going to be quite a big bag and there was very little rubbish so far as they could tell.

All the scuppers had been blocked from one end of the deck to the other, which was just as well, for the second Henry snatched the cod end slip knot, shrimps shot everywhere. Laurie had never seen the catch so alive. Shrimps were bouncing so high along the deck, one or two even jumped back overboard. They were a wonderful sight, so alive and so vital, full of energy. Laurie thought how sad that within a few minutes some of them would be in the copper, boiled alive.

When the haul had been completely sorted, there were twelve skate, one small box of plaice, and fifty gallons of the biggest and most gorgeous pink shrimps Laurie had ever seen. One of the strangest things about creatures of the sea is how they change colour when cooked. When shrimps first came on board they were almost a transparent white, yet now as they lay cooling, after being cooked, the process had turned them into a beautiful deep pinky red. It made Laurie's mouth water, just to look at them.

They made two more hauls that day before heading for home, neither being quite so lucrative as the first, but making a very satisfactory day's work, one to be enjoyed and remembered.

As so often happens after a fine spell of continuous calm weather, it broke up with a fresh easterly wind, which, although hardly noticeable on land, can be very uncomfortable at sea.

Having been more than satisfied with the previous day's work, the *The Valory* was once more heading for the pink shrimp grounds, but minus one of her crew. Today, Peter and Laurie were on their own, and they were getting a very unwelcome early morning shake up from swell caused by the easterly wind, against a strong ebb tide.

There had been a short discussion regarding conditions and the distance involved, considering it was going to be a head punch all the way, but they had decided to risk it. With any luck, as tide eased, so should the swell.

Just at this moment, the boys were doubting their judgment. *The Valory* was thoroughly enjoying herself, behaving like a bucking bronco. She crashed through the broken water, throwing spray from stem to stern. Her complete disregard of the resistance being offered by the elements, proved what a sturdy little ship she was, but the disturbance did not go down very well with egg and bacon, as Peter soon found out. Early morning was not one of his best times, but they pressed on.

When they eventually reached the grounds and shot away, less than half of those boats present on the previous day, had arrived, it appeared they had decided that the conditions would not be suitable. Not many fishermen of those days, favoured an easterly wind.

Peter and Laurie were to learn another very important lesson that day. As it turned out, the fishing was not particularly good, The boys were to say the least a bit disappointed.

As they had expected, by the time tide had eased, it was almost a flat calm, but the fishing was poor. The water was thick and sandy coloured , In four separate one hour hauls, they had barely mustered thirty gallons of pink shrimps, and it was only on the last haul, before going home, that they added a few skate and plaice to the tally.

They went alongside two of the other boats and were met with the same story. Fishing had been poor all the way round, as one old fisherman, who came from a different port, put it, "What else would you expect with such bloody awful conditions, they should have stayed at home." The shrimps were there, because they were crawling or laying all over the back of the net, but very few reached the cod end bag. His description of an easterly wind was less than complimentary, in fact unprintable!

Laurie was finished cooking long before they reached home. When the shrimps had cooled and been put into sacks, Laurie, who had been giving a lot of thought to the day's fishing, walked aft to have a chat with Peter and compare thoughts. This was a practice which conjured up many ideas and bore much fruit in their life at sea together.

Laurie asked Peter what specific thing had struck him most about the fishing that day.

It was almost as if they could read each other's minds. Peter's answer confirmed that his mind was on the same wavelength. "You mean about the shrimps being everywhere but down inside the net?" Laurie nodded, and suggested that it might be one of two things. Either the gear had been unsteady on the bottom, because of the swell, which was most unlikely as it had died down on the low water, or the shrimps were swimming higher than the head rope and above the trawl beam level.

Peter was in complete agreement, he was quite sure the disturbance had caused the shrimps to swim higher than the gear could reach, but as the height of the net head line was controlled by the trawlheads at each end, what could they do about making it higher without pulling the gear to pieces?

Laurie had already thought about this and made a suggestion.

His idea was to drill down through the wooden beam at either end, close to the trawlhead. Put a fifteen inch long eye bolt through each hole and run the head line through the eyes, so lifting it some ten inches. If this made any difference at all, maybe they could improve on this with something more permanent.

Peter was in full agreement, dashing off as soon as they reached the shore, to collect his motor bike and gather the bits that were needed.

The next day, when they put to sea, it was rigged, ready for use.

Conditions on the following day were identical. Once again the *The Valory* gave them a rough ride down through the middle of a very turbulent channel. Whoever stood at the helm received a good soaking, but at least the water was warm. Had it been winter, the experience would have been most unpleasant, but in summer, no more than a good wash, even if one did have their clothes on. Only one other boat had bothered to muster, but he was one of the best fishermen around at that time. Both Peter and Laurie were pleased to see him, they needed a comparison for their experiment. If anything, there appeared to be a little more swell than the previous day, in fact, the first haul was very lumpy. Even with the gear overboard, it was still difficult to get a cup of tea from forward to aft, without losing most of it.

Both boats were shot away within ten minutes of each other. It was useless working the try net in such rough conditions. Today would just be pot luck, a forty minute tow and then haul. It was going to be a hard pull, with just the two crew - they were going to miss Henry today.

Hauling turned out to be harder than they expected. The lifted headline appeared to make more flow of water through the net, but at least they could see it was all intact. The bolts had not bent and they could see shrimps shooting around everywhere.

Even before the ground rope was aboard, they could tell that the cod end was heavier than usual, the signs were good, it was movable, not dead weight. When at last they managed to get the strop and tackle hoist on the cod end, the bag was so big that for the first time on the *The Valory*, they had to use a double part hoist, which doubled the lifting power - it was an enormous bag.

Fortunately the swell had gradually decreased. Peter gave the engine one good thrust ahead, with the helm hard over, which brought the sturdy little ship stern to the wind, just as the huge bag of shrimps slid over onto the deck. Whatever happened now, this one haul contained a day's work, they might not even need to shoot again.

When Peter pulled the slip knot on the cod end tyre, it was as if the whole deck became alive, shrimps kicked everywhere, sliding and jumping into every spare nook and cranny they could find. It was a wonderful sight to behold, just one of nature's many great thrills which Peter and Laurie were destined to enjoy together in their fishing life. They had been so absorbed in their efforts, that it was only now, as they stood back grinning at each other, they noticed the other shrimp boat. She had come close enough for the skipper, who had seen the enormous bag, to enquire if they were in trouble.

But he had no need to ask, the decks full of shrimps, were clearly visible for all to see. He scratched his head in disbelief, he had not even filled two five gallon baskets.

It appeared that the little modification had worked beyond all their wildest dreams.

CHAPTER FIFTY EIGHT

That experiment carried out on the pink shrimp fishing was typical of the way progress was made at that time. Everything was a case of trial and error, Fishermen were very secretive about changes they made in the nets and attachments relating to the gear being used, and even more important, the ground which was gradually opened up once again after the war.

It would be no exaggeration to estimate that it cost fishermen of every country, millions of pounds in lost and damaged gear, and clearing up the mess which had been left behind.

Few people would know about or could imagine how many lives were lost or the number of fishermen crippled and maimed, retrieving objects of all descriptions, left behind on the sea bed.

Almost every day a boat suffered damage or wreckage got caught in the nets, to be brought ashore or dumped at sea on a recognized dumping ground, depending on how heavy or dangerous the object was.

One such incident happened about this time when some twelve boats were working in an area already mentioned. It eventually became known, and marked on the charts, as numerous wrecks.

When boats were at work in an area of this description, it became customary to keep a sharp lookout, and take note of when any one boat stopped unexpectedly or appeared to be in trouble.

When this situation arose, land marks or compass bearings

would immediately be taken, and if the vessel concerned came round head to tide and stayed in the one position for a period of time, vessels close by would automatically haul in their gear and hasten to offer assistance.

On the day in question, one boat had stopped but remained stern to tide and stayed that way. The other boats took marks and bearings as usual, but kept the vessel under observation. It became obvious that something quite serious was wrong, when a flag appeared at the masthead. Several boats instantly hauled their trawls and steamed with all speed back over tide to the stricken vessel.

She was in serious trouble, making water rapidly. While towing along with tide behind her, the little boat had run onto a piece of submerged wreckage, piercing its way up through her planking, as she settled in the water.

It was a risky thing to do, but two of the vessels which had answered her distress signals, immediately breasted up on either side, to prevent her from sinking any further, but as the tide still had an hour to ebb, they could not prevent the stump entering even further into her hull, Without lifting her completely out of the water, and this was beyond their capability. Fortunately, she was one of the smallest shrimp boats, and once the tackle was rigged, they managed to hold her perched up on top of the stump until low water. Many possible dangers faced the rescuers, but once they were all lashed alongside, those involved were fully committed to a complete salvage operation. All thoughts of fishing at that moment gone from their minds.

First hand knowledge of the dramatic rescue that was taking place only four miles away, came to the *The Valory* as she was working her way towards home on the flood tide.

Tide had just turned, as one of the boats which had been standing by at the scene of the rescue, came alongside in search of hacksaw blades.

The skipper of the vessel told how he had steamed round the whole fleet on his mission, and that their were nine hands aboard the damaged shrimp boat, taking turns at cutting through the stump, which had pierced the hull to a depth of five feet.

The rescue plan was to cut some three feet off the stump in order to lift the boat clear, before tide rose too high, and became strong enough to create more problems or cause more damage. Hopefully, if they could achieve this, she would be saved.

While explanations were being made, Laurie had found a new packet of blades in the engine room tool box, and handed them over.

Within the hour, every boat in the fleet was at the scene, ready to assist if they were needed.

Fortunately, the weather was fine and calm, if it had been otherwise, all efforts to save the boat would surely have failed, but the rescue was a success.

On the flood tide, with a whole convoy of vessels in attendance, the little shrimp boat was lifted safely off the wreck and towed home, much to the relief of the skipper.

Laurie was to see and be involved in many such incidents during his life as a fisherman, but on this occasion they had lost only an hour's work. It occurred to him as they made their way home; that many of those who helped on that day, could hardly afford to lose the fishing time, let alone the risk of damaging their own vessels, but at sea, all else was forgotten in times of trouble - money became unimportant.

CHAPTER FIFTY NINE

When *Reindeer* and *The Valory* landed that day, there, standing proudly waiting for them, was the old green Ford box wagon. Today she was to be commissioned for the first time.

If the vehicle waiting on the quay had been a silver Rolls Royce, it could not have caused more excitement, After all she did cost eighty pounds and that was big money: By the time they had landed and loaded the catch, Father had not put in an appearance, which was most unusual. His reputation for selling fish and shrimps straight off the boats, had spread far and wide, and in fact became a legend in his own lifetime, but at the moment he was no where to be seen.

Ray served the customers who were waiting, while his brothers prepared the van for its short journey up to the yard.

When they were ready, Father had still not put in an appearance. The brothers were anxious to be away, there were still many jobs to be completed before they could go home.

They knew Father would not approve, but after some debate, it was decided that as Peter had a motor bike licence, he should be first to drive the van. The old wagon's engine started first turn on the handle, they were ready to go, but not at the speed Peter wanted to drive. They shot round the sea wall as if it were a race track. Peter thought he was still driving his motor bike.

Fishermen standing on the quay leapt for safety as the old green wagon was thrown into contortions which she had never been built for.

Cars on the sea front reverently gave way, as the missile flashed past, seemingly hell bent on destruction.

There were just two corners to navigate, the first would take them off the sea front, and was a left hand turn. The brothers inside were thrown into a confused mixed heap of shrimps and bodies, as the corner was taken without slackening speed. The driving door flew open, almost hitting a police car which had come to a halt at the corner, but was fortunately going in the opposite direction.

Fishermen onlookers, telling the story years later, swore that the van went round the corner on two wheels. It all happened so fast that even the police car failed to track them down.

The old green wagon had been introduced to a new way of life, and this was the first of the horrifying experiences which she was forced to endure in the next few years.

They did arrive at the yard without killing anyone, much to the surprise of everyone concerned.

A not very happy looking Father witnessed the arrival, as the van came to a halt with screeching of tyres. Peter was not very popular once again.

Many amazing and some times hair raising experiences were to take place in the next few months of Laurie's life. The old green box wagon was to feature in quite a number. In a way, it became another member of the family and developed in character accordingly.

So far as the Gilson family were concerned, she was a lovable old toy, but also a very important part of the business. It is possible, However, That in some quarters of Laurie's home town, the *Green Flash*, as somebody once called her, was considered a menace. Whenever she appeared on the quay with any one of the brothers driving, she was always treated with the greatest respect. Local fishermen allowed her plenty of room to manoeuvre, they never forgot that first home run.

Laurie was to play a part in two other rather dramatic happenings, both of which could have proved disastrous, if fate had not decreed otherwise. The winter of his seventeenth birthday was almost upon them. Nature took its normal course, as the water temperature dropped, so shrimps became scarce and demand increased.

Father had managed to get the old *Lady D* back into some semblance of seaworthiness, deciding that they should make an attempt to work three boats. He considered her capable of working the grounds within a radius of ten miles, if the weather was reasonable.

Having once made the decision, Father elected himself as skipper and Laurie was seconded as mate.

Laurie had no reservations about working with Father, but the *Lady D* was definitely a step down the ladder, she really was past it.

On the first morning she put to sea, they had problems starting the engine. It was supposed to start on petrol, then change over to paraffin when sufficiently hot, but the carburettor kept flooding, and even when they did get started, the engine would only run on petrol. Every time Father turned over to paraffin, she would start to splutter. Eventually they did manage to get under way, deciding to let the engine stay on petrol, if that was the only way they were going to get a day's work.

Once the deck had been prepared for work, Laurie went down into the cabin to make some tea, it would take them almost an hour to reach the grounds and he had plenty of time.

First of all, the little primus stove used for boiling the kettle, refused to work, Then when the problem was cured, Laurie found that the kettle leaked badly. Luckily he managed to find a saucepan, which he filled and put on the stove, he then sat back, waiting for it to boil.

It was fortunate that Laurie was not the nervous type. Everything he had done had been carried out in semi-darkness. Now, as he spread his hands out on either side, he could feel the old timbers, rough to the touch, and very damp, but there was something else.'

A soft slithering sound, which he could not place, came to his ears, then the hairs on the back of his neck began to tingle as claws attempted to grip his right hand. He could not see what it was, but he could feel the slime dropping from the creature (whatever it was) and running down his arm.

With his heart thumping, Laurie made one mad grab for the top of the claws, and then began to laugh out loud with relief - it was only an oil covered crab which had crawled up out of the bilges . He took it up on deck to show Father, the poor old thing must have been living down there for months.

They only just had time to finish their tea before shooting the gear. Laurie had a feeling it was going to be one of those days.

No sooner was the trawl on the sea bed and the warp made fast, when suddenly the engine room bilges burst into flame and a blast of scorching heat came rushing up through the hatch.

Laurie was on his way aft, when it happened, he saw Father unclip the pyrene extinguisher, which had hung on the back of the hatch for years, and breaking the seal, began pumping frantically down into the engine room. Laurie grabbed the dip bucket, and began throwing water inside the hatch, but not toward the engine. Then Father did something which could have cost him his life.

The flames appeared to die down a little and Father attempted to look down into the engine room, The fumes knocked him out cold, He almost choked to death. Laurie dragged him away from the hatch, luckily the pyrene extinguisher had done its work and the fire went out, but it had been a close call. Ten minutes passed before Father recovered enough to speak. In that time Laurie had removed both their water boots, Just in case they had to swim for it.

That almost disastrous day signalled the end of two very important factors in the life of Laurie and his family.

The *Lady D* carried just one sail, called a sampan. It was similar to those used aboard Chinese junks, not very big, but quite efficient.

Having first checked that the fire was out completely, and soaking with water any wood which was still smouldering, Laurie made sure Father was comfortable, he had been badly shaken and even now sat leaning against the cabin hatch, With a dazed look on his face It was obvious that they would not be fishing any more today, and so far as the old *Lady D* was concerned possibly never again, but now he had the problem of recovering the trawl alone. Laurie knew he was capable of the task, but it was going to take time and energy. Energy was one resource of which Laurie had plenty in reserve.

Almost an hour had passed by the time he had secured the last lashing but it had been accomplished with very little fuss. He now turned his attention to the sampan sail. Having hoisted the canvas many times in the past, it was purely routine, but as he was working alone, he took that extra care, they had experienced more than enough trouble for one day.

Sailing the *Lady D* home was a mere formality. The light breeze which came from a south westerly direction, was all she needed to bring her gently back into Southend.

Laurie was more concerned about Father than the boat. By the time they had berthed alongside, he was sufficiently recovered to move about the deck. He had been sick several times, and this appeared to have cleared his system. He suffered no lasting injury, but that was the last serious day's fishing of his life.

CHAPTER SIXTY

The new boat for Ray was now nearing completion, and a launching date was being discussed for the *Boy John*. She was not very big, only thirty two feet in length, and eleven feet beam, but probably one of the strongest and best built boats of her time.

The boatyard where she was built had originally worked on many of the commercial sailing barges which traded on the River Thames, and it was often said of her that she was built like a barge and just as strong - her life was about to begin.

A new boat coming into the fleet, and one of the oldest skippers about to retire, but not quite, Father did make a small comeback, if only for a few days.

Partly due to the new boat being almost completed, but also brought about by a certain amount of friction between the brothers. The crew situation became a little confused over the next couple of months. Laurie found himself being switched from one boat to another as the days progressed.

How it came about, he was not quite sure, After the fire aboard *Lady D* put her once more out of commission, Laurie got shipped back aboard *Reindeer* with Henry. Most of these situations were temporary, but also a little bit unsettling. He loved having a routine to work with and all of his brothers had different ways.

In those days, Laurie was prepared to work when and wherever he was needed. The weather was cold but fine. *Reindeer* was fishing on very rough ground known as the Boulders.

The very nature of this area prevented hauls from lasting more than thirty or forty minutes, because of the possibility that rocks would be picked up and the net torn to pieces.

They had already completed two hauls, without mishap, The fishing had been good but on the third haul they struck real trouble. The net was barely halfway up, already they could tell that the weight was more than fish.

It took some time to get the cod end and bag alongside and slung on the tackle. Even then, it needed the double part as well.

Laurie had some doubt that they would be able to lift the bag aboard even with the double part on, but they were going to try.

Both brothers put all their weight on the tackle rope, and gradually the big bag of rocks and fish came out of the water and slid up *Reindeer's* side. It stopped about six inches short, they had reached maximum height.

They had a short discussion and decided that with one pulling on the cod end tyre, and the other putting his shoulder against the bag and pushing, they should manage to roll the bag aboard.

Laurie braced himself with his left foot against a timberhead, ready to pull. Henry put his shoulder against the bag and together exerted all their strength. The bag moved, and had just cleared the topside ready to drop on the deck, when there was a sharp crack, the tackle top pennant had snapped and the bag crashed onto the deck. Henry, with all his weight pushing out-board, stood no chance of saving himself from going overboard. In just a split second, the only part of Henry showing, was the sole of his boots, the rest was submerged. Fortunately for Henry, the bag had landed on the deck, had it gone overboard and the net sunk away, almost certainly he would have been pulled under at the same time. Laurie hanging overboard, Grabbed one of the boots and pulled. He had never before realized how heavy a body became when fully clothed, and sodden with water.

First, the top of his boots, then an arm appeared, as Henry threshed about, trying to get his head above water. Then at last Laurie managed to get hold of his hair, and he came up spitting and coughing, gasping for breath. Henry was saved and none the worse for his ducking but it was touch and go, the story might well have had a very different ending.

CHAPTER SIXTY ONE

The next time Laurie put to sea in the *Reindeer*, he was surprised that Father was aboard with him.

He had prepared the deck as usual, washing boxes, putting fuel in the tanks and getting the net ready to shoot away.

He had just made a cup of tea and taken one aft for Father, who was standing at the helm. They discussed where would be the best place to fish that day and why. Then Laurie got the surprise of his life. Father, stepping away from the helm said "Take her Lol, you appear to think the day through as well as anyone I know, from now on she's yours, and I'll be your mate."

Laurie was speechless. All kinds of questions flashed through his mind at that moment.

It was one thing to talk about where and how you were going to fish, but a completely different matter if you had the last word, and then carried the responsibility of putting that word into action. For a long time now, Laurie had formed a mental log of each area fished and how well it would yield. His experience increased with every day. He welcomed the challenge and the excitement bubbled over inside, at the prospect of all his dreams coming true. All he had to do now was prove his capability.

Laurie went through that first day as skipper, in a kind of trance. He only once digressed from the normal routine, It cost two hours fishing time but yielded eighty large skate. Laurie was well pleased, and although Father said nothing, his smile of approval was enough. It was a day for Laurie to remember in so many ways. His life as a real hunting fisherman had commenced,The battle was really on.

There were more surprises to come later that evening after they had landed.

Without a moment to spare, Laurie jumped on his bike and dashed off to tell Doris that he was now officially skipper of the *Reindeer* He arrived at the house, to be allowed over the threshold by Doris's grandmother, Who made it very obvious that she had many reservations about him.

Doris's parents were out, and for the first time she had been given permission to prepare Laurie a meal, normally she was never allowed in the kitchen.

This question of a daughter of the house, never being allowed to use all the facilities which were essential for acquiring the arts of cooking, puzzled Laurie. Doris's mother had become a great ally, even if he did tease her something terrible. She had her funny little ways, but they were now close friends and she usually came out on his side if an argument did occur. Nevertheless, in that tiny kitchen she was determined to reign supreme, and all the teasing in the world was not going to move her.

Having been brought up in a large family where everyone fought for survival, and often left to fend for themselves, Laurie could cook almost anything. Often at sea, If you refused to cook, you didn't eat, it was all part of the job.

Now as Laurie climbed the stairs, and grandmother (making some adverse comment about young people being left on their own) returned to her downstairs flat. He wondered just how well Doris would cope. She was in the kitchen with the door ajar, and he could hear her singing as he made his way through the dining room, all appeared to be under control. The gas stove in that kitchen was a monstrosity. It was very old and should have been thrown out years before. It had a habit of going out when turned onto the low mark, and was extremely dangerous. At that moment Doris had food in the oven with the gas (as she thought) on low but the flame had gone out and the hob on top was still burning!

It all happened in a split second, as Laurie pulled back the kitchen door, Doris opened the oven and was instantly enveloped in a sheet of flame. She fell back against the food cupboard with a frightened cry, hands thrown up to protect her face. Laurie could see the tongues of fire licking at her hair. Perhaps for the first time in his life he was thankful that constant strain and salt water, had made his hands so large. They covered Doris's head, smothering the menacing flame.

Fortunately Doris was not seriously hurt. Now, as she lay in Laurie's arms, with only the fire throwing its light onto the small living room walls, her sobbing gradually subsided and all was still - food had been forgotten, For the moment time was of no importance, In the silence of that moment Laurie knew that the girl now resting safely in his arms, would one day be his wife.

Letting his thoughts wander over the years which had brought him to this point of his life. He realized how fortunate he had been. All those dreams of adventure were coming true.

Looking down at his thick, powerful arms, reminded him of the fragile, puny boy who had made that horrible train journey to the Midlands, just nine short years ago - it hardly seemed possible. He would never allow those early days of misery to be erased from his memory.

He recalled the wonder and beauty of the canal, the fun and excitement, the pranks and mischief.

That special relationship with Rita, which seamed a lifetime back into the past.

Then Mr. Jones, the teacher, who in Laurie's most desperate hour of need, had come to his rescue, pulling him out of a world of mental darkness, in that far off Midland Town.

The past ran through his mind like a dream, intermingled with the future and all its possibilities. The gates of adventure were now wide open to him. The sea was his life. But even that would have to wait for the moment, Doris was pulling him back to the present - she wanted to be kissed!

Another time, another life, my world 1941

Tranquillity, absolute paradise, Heaven on earth

*The Ros Beara, Author's Ship for the last twenty years of his life at sea,
Purchased Greencastle Southern Ireland 1960*

Dalriada (Skipper Steve Gilson) purchased North Shields 1978

Vessel De-Hoop (Skipper Bill Gilson) purchased Holland Yerseke 1972

Converted canal barge

'If you can make a living fishing in the Thames Estuary you'd make a fortune anywhere else.'

At the helm, skipper Laurie Gilson . . . on the deck, mate Derek Tyrrell sorts the catch

Believed to be one of the first publications of the Evening Echo October 6th 1969. Author at the helm of the Ros beara. Plenty of fish, life at its very best.

Paul Gilson, Paul Manners, Steve Noakes, sorting the catch on board the Ros Beara.

*Up round the Kneck in fish aboard the fishing vessel Anja
purchased by the author from Holland 1972*

Author mending a hole in the cod-end of the net, a task that never ends.
Very good for the nerves, when one wants to meditate

Showing off the prime while the fish are still kicking.
Always a thrilling moment.

Authors Grandson and name-sake, eighteen year old Laurence.
Shaking soles out of the cod end.

Steve Gilson, authors son and father of Laurence, heaving up on the dolly

Top Cod-end full of Dover-Sole stickers waiting to be shaken out and gutted.

Wreck of the ammunition ship Montgomery, back broken across a sand-bank and doomed to stay until she disappears out of sight into the sea-bed.

A good big bag of mixed species of fish that would warm the cockles of any true fishermans heart.

How Southend stays top of the trawl

FEW Southenders realise that their town is the top fishing centre in Essex and Kent. Investment in modern aids has meant increasingly profitable catches. DAVID CREWE spent a day on one of Southend's up-to-date trawlers. Here is his report.

THE saying goes that if you can make a living fishing in the Thames Estuary, you can make a fortune doing it anywhere else.

And after watching some of Southend's fishing fleet at work I can believe it.

For the men who last year made it top fishing centre in Essex and Kent have got the toughest job in the region.

Just after full tide at two o'clock one morning, with a cold wind whipping up the crests of the inkblack waves, I boarded an open motor-boat at the landing stage east of Southend pier.

Standing at the tiller was Laurie Gilson, 37-year-old skipper of the 24-ton fishing boat Ross Beora, lying nearly a mile away at anchor in the deep water of the Ray. His mate, Derek Tyrrell, 31, stood beside him, hands in pockets, eyeing sky and sea.

□ □

Laurie Gilson has been at sea since he was 14 and is the youngest brother of a family combine which dominates fishing in Southend.

They own seven boats, invest in the most modern scientific aids, and the profit from everything they catch goes into a kitty to be shared out.

Ross Beora, one of the two bigger ships of their fleet, bought secondhand from Ireland 18 months ago for about £6,000, has just been fitted with radar in addition to her echo sounder — which doubles as a depth-finder and fishfinder — and radio-telephone.

Our journey to the boat was the first of the many difficulties the fishermen have to face.

As there is no deep-water harbour in Southend heavier draught vessels have to be moored well offshore in the Ray. To get to the boat and back adds two hours to what is already a long working day — and reduces fishing time.

□ □

But once aboard, the eight-cylinder Gardiner marine engine soon had us under way, headed for the open water at the mouth of the estuary.

With the skipper at the wheel, using the lights of the shore as bearings to keep the winding channel, Derek Tyrrell began to check the trawl nets, winches and hawsers.

In the wheelhouse, the radio telephone and the radar filled the air with electronic buzzing. The pierhead, empty deckchairs illuminated by navigation warning lights,

came and went. Course was set along a line of flashing marker buoys.

"You can imagine it in the winter," said Laurie. "That's when we get our really big hauls of sprats and cod. The decks and equipment are covered with frost or snow and there is an icy wind.

"After a week of fishing you are completely flaked out and you don't feel much like socialising."

Most trips take 12 hours from tide to tide, but the two bigger boats — with their larger holds — often stay out for 24 hours. Ross Beora has bunk space below and a small coal-stove for warmth.

The fishing grounds we were heading for were right in the big ship lanes. Dozens of cargo vessels were anchored each side of the lanes, waiting for the tide, or a pilot — or just passing time.

□ □

And just as a faint red streak of dawn tinged the sky in the east, and the wind stiffened, the first trawl began in about ten fathoms of choppy water.

The net went over with a splash. We were fishing for flatfish — sole and plaice. The trawl stays down for more than an hour.

As the sun moved off the horizon, the trawl was brought in. The winches bit against the hawsers and finally the net was hauled aboard.

A cascade of fish, crabs, starfish, seaweed, stones and shells fell on to the decking when the bottom of the net was released.

Dover soles, plaice and flounders were tossed into boxes. The rest went overboard.

There did not seem much left, but Derek had been selective and the fish that stared coldly from the boxes were big and plump.

By the time we were heading back to Southend, ten hours had passed and about ten stone of fish were stowed in boxes, gutted and washed.

"Ten stone is a fair day's work for us," explained Laurie. "We must clear between £18 and £20 a day to pay for the running of the boat. All this fish will be sold in our own shop.

□ □

"In winter when we get our big hauls of cod, sprats and herring — the net sometimes weighs more than a ton — they are sold on the market at Billingsgate. Some go to Southend shops."

On shore the Gilsons have a manager who takes care of marketing the catches and all the bookwork involved.

"You can't do this job at all if you have got any worries," he said. "You are so cut off from everything that any troubles prey on your mind. I have been lucky and had a settled home life."

Compared with the giant fishing fleets of Grimsby, Hull, Fleetwood and Aberdeen, the fishermen of Southend are small fry. They measure their yearly catch in stones, not tons. They measure their trips in hours, not days.

But they share the same sort of tough conditions, strain and foul weather. In the food getting business — man's oldest — fishermen are the only hunters left.

The publishing of this book has been delayed nineteen years to save any embarrassment it might have caused for my brothers who have now sadly all passed away.

My three books:
"Magic Of the Waterways" Now hopefully published,
"Challenge Of The Sea" Already published
"Harvest of the Sea" Yet to be written

I hope the best is yet to come

L G Gilson